PRESENTATION

Patrimonio Nacional (National Heritage) is the institution which manages those properties of the State which are at the service of the Crown for performing representative functions as commended by the Constitution and Laws of Spain.

The institution manages a number of Palaces, as well as several Monasteries and Convents founded by Spanish monarchs, all of great historical, artistic and cultural importance and, most significantly, of great *symbolic value*. The Royal Palaces of Madrid, El Pardo, Aranjuez, San Ildefonso and La Almudaina are used as residential and representative buildings as was intended when they were built centuries ago and it is here where His Majesty the King performs his duties as Head of State, particularly in the Royal Palace of Madrid, where this *symbolic value* is felt most strongly, as the official residence of the Crown.

In harmony with these functions, the other buildings and properties which make up Patrimonio Nacional have a decidedly cultural purpose and are places of study and research, as well as being open to the general public.

Both the buildings and the Spanish royal collections (27 in all, ranging from fans to tools and which include silverware, paintings, tapestries, furniture, musical instruments, clocks, etc.) are remarkable for a number of characteristics which go to make Patrimonio Nacional a unique cultural institution: their *particular purpose*, as they are still considered valid for representative use by the Crown; their *historical authenticity*, as they are all pieces which have been ordered, acquired or offered as gifts at some time for that particular place; their *originality*, which can be seen by the absence of replicas and imitations, and their *extraordinary artistic, historical and symbolic value*.

The combination of such impressive characteristics makes it clear to the visitor that Patrimonio Nacional is much more than a simple museum.

The Spanish Royal Palaces are surrounded by approximately 20,500 hectares of open land. Around 500 hectares are given over to gardens or farmland, while the remaining 20,000 hectares are forest, divided between El Pardo, La Herrería and Riofrío and part of which is open to the general public. These woodlands, mainly of the biotype *Mediterranean forest*, are of renowned ecological importance, the value of which is at a par with the monuments found in their midst.

The Royal Monasteries and Convents have been attended by the same religious orders since their foundation, with the exception of San Lorenzo de El Escorial, originally of the Hieronymite Order, which was passed over to the Augustinian Order following the sale of Church lands in the 19th century. They enjoy particular importance in the history of Spain, as their origin dates back to the particular patronage of the monarchs of the era.

By being open to the general public, not only do these buildings fulfil a cultural purpose, they allow the Spanish people to capture their symbolic value, identify with it and consider themselves a legatee of the vast historical and artistic treasures which make up the properties of Patrimonio Nacional.

Collected over the centuries by the Crown, their influence in the cultural identity of Spain has been, and still is, decisive.

© EDITORIAL PATRIMONIO NACIONAL. 1996

Palacio Real de Madrid

Bailén, s/n

28071 MADRID

Tel. 91 547.53.50

© ALDEASA. 1996

© Of all texts: José Luis Sancho Gaspar

N.I.P.O. 006-98-007-7

Depósito Legal: M-18383-1998

I.S.B.N. 84-7120-219-0

I.S.B.N. 84-8003-092-5

Coordination: Aldeasa, Patrimonio Nacional

Design and Layout: Myriam López Consalvi

Translation: Mervyn Samuel

Photographs: Patrimonio Nacional, Félix Lorrio, Ramón Guerra, Antonio Sanz, Gerardo Romera

Photomechanics: Lucam

Cover illustration: View of the main façade of the Royal Palace, Madrid, from the *Lithographic Collection of Views of the Royal Seats*, by Fernando Brambilla, 1832.

Printed by: Estudios Gráficos Europeos S. A., Madrid

Printed in Spain.

April 1998

VISITOR'S GUIDE

ROYAL PALACE
OF MADRID

José Luis Sancho

CONTENTS

INTRODUCTION

FROM FORTRESS TO PALACE

The Royal Palace is on the site where once stood the Alcázar of Madrid, the "famous castle" built at the end of the 9th century, during the reign of Mohammed I, Emir of Córdoba, as a key position for the defence of these territories situated to the north of Toledo.

The fortress, rebuilt in the 14th century, acquired the character of a royal residence with the work undertaken by John II, particularly the chapel consecrated in 1434, and the great "rich hall". It was in the 16th century that Charles V and Philip II rebuilt it as a Royal Palace, so that in 1561 the Alcázar became the permanent residence of the Kings, and the *"villa"* or town of Madrid which arose under the protection of its castle became the Court of the Spanish Monarchy. Under Philip IV, the Palace attained its most characteristic form: on the exterior, with the long façade designed by Francisco and Juan Gómez de Mora and G. B. Crescenci; on the interior, with the participation of Diego Velázquez as interior-design architect and with the display of masterpieces which today are the pride of the Prado Museum. Philip V also left his mark on the Alcázar before the greatest and best part of its structure disappeared in a fire on the Christmas Eve of 1734.

The location of the Alcázar and its groundplan, conceived around the buildings containing the living quarters, in such a way conditioned the shape of the New Royal Palace and its setting that we could almost claim that it is still present today, despite the disappearance of all visible remains in the area.

The Royal Seats

The fact that Madrid, and more accurately the Alcázar or Royal Palace, was the seat of power, did not mean that the King lived only in this Palace. The game reserves near Madrid used by the Trastamara dynasty (El Pardo, Valsaín), the domain of Aranjuez incorporated into the Crown by the Catholic Monarchs, the Monastery of El Escorial founded by Philip II, and other possessions also created by the latter Monarch (especially the neighbouring Casa de Campo, on the other side of the Manzanares), constituted a system of "Royal Seats" defined at the time when the capital was established here. During the following three centuries it was extended and improved with new Royal Seats, such as the Buen Retiro and La Granja de San Ildefonso, creations of Philip IV and Philip V respectively. The use of these residences was seasonal, according to their nature and characteristics: springtime was spent at Aranjuez, summer at Valsaín (from the time of Philip V at the nearby La Granja), autumn at El Escorial... The Monarchs stayed in Madrid from the end of October until Holy Week, but with prolonged stays at the winter hunting lodge of El Pardo. Philip V, and particularly Charles III, took this systematic absence from the capital to its ultimate consequences. This system did not always function in a strict manner, but though it was subject to exceptions, novelties and changes imposed by the preferences of each Monarch,

The Palace in the City

"The Palace itself stands in one of the few fine situations the city affords; being placed on a considerable eminence overlooking the least uninteresting side of the country..."
ANONYMOUS: *Spain, Tangier, etc., visited in 1840 and 1841. By X.Y.Z.* London, 1845.

"The palace is a noble building of white stone, occupying a commanding situation, and looks very imposing from a distance." Louisa Mary Anne TENISON: *Castile and Andalucia*. London, 1853.

"This is certainly one of the most magnificent royal residences in the world, imposing in itself, and striking from its position at the end of the finest part of the town, on the edge of a steep bank." Augustus John Cuthbert HARE: *Wanderings in Spain*, London, 1873.

The west façade of the Palace, facing towards the river, from the Park or Campo del Moro.

The Alcázar in the time of Philip II. Detail of painting by Alonso Sánchez Coello. Convent of Las Descalzas Reales. Madrid.

Juvarra and his Project

"It is said that the Minister Campillo, to support his political or economic objectives, or both at the same time, prevented the grand project of Don Filippo Juvarra from being carried out, an undertaking considered capable of emptying even the treasure chests of the Spanish Monarch. Such extremely vast plans would be drawn from his no less vast mind by Don Filippo, whose designs on a page certainly cost him less than the charge they would mean to others when built on a square."
Fr.Norberto CAIMO (the Italian wanderer): *Voyage d'Espagne, fait en l'année 1755... Paris, 1772-1773.*

"A mahogany model of the projected palace is still shown in Madrid, and must of itself have cost the price of as good a dwelling as any modest man need wish for. This palace was to have lodged the royal body guard, the ministers, tribunals and indeed every thing connected with the machine of state. Alexander Slidell MACKENZIE: *A year in Spain, by a young American.*
London, 1831.

Detail of main façade of Juvarra's project for the Royal Palace of Madrid.

the fact is that for three centuries it governed the life of the Spanish Court, the main axis of which was the Palace of Madrid.

The New Royal Palace

Almost as soon as the fire of that Christmas Eve of 1734 was extinguished, Philip V decided to build a new Royal Palace in Madrid, and to do so on the very same site where the former one had stood, as a symbol of the continuity of the Monarchy. He wanted the entire structure to have stone vaulting, with timber being employed only for doors and window-frames, in order to avoid further fires. There may also have been a desire to identify the solidity of the seat with that of power: the inscription on the foundation stone states that it was built "for eternity". The Palace needed space for all the functions of the Court, one of the most important in Europe at that time. Moreover, this was precisely the moment when ideas regarding the splendour that should surround regal power were reaching their maximum expression.

ARCHITECTURE: PROJECTS AND CONSTRUCTION

Philip V also wanted the architect of his Palace to be the best and most famous one in Europe, and he chose well. At the beginning of 1735, the Italian Filippo Juvarra was summoned to Madrid. He quickly realized that the location of the Alcázar was not appropriate for a residence as large and magnificent as was intended, and he conceived a vast project with horizontal development, much more suitable for a flat site. However, Juvarra died in March 1736, and being delighted with his style the Monarchs decided to call on a disciple of his to build the master's great project.

So it was that G. B. Sacchetti, of Turin, came to Madrid, and was commissioned to "adapt" Juvarra's design to the site of the old Palace, which was no easy matter. He had neither the prestige nor the personality of Juvarra, and as he was in no position to object, he obeyed.

The final form of the Palace is the result of a complex process, the basic elements of which are the plans of Juvarra, the adaptation of these in what really was a completely new project by Sacchetti, and modifications of many aspects introduced during construction. Finally, there were the changes introduced into the Palace of Sacchetti by Sabatini, architect of Charles III.

The architectural design of the Palace, in its general features and its details, is characteristic of the classical late-Baroque taste of Juvarra, chiefly inspired by the famous Roman artist Bernini, and it follows the lines of the great project that never became a reality. However, Sacchetti had to convert the original horizontal conception into a vertical design so that, occupying the same site as the old Alcázar, the New Palace would be able to accomodate the Royal Family, courtiers, servants, ministries and service quarters. Thus, the building has a minimum of six storeys and a maximum of eight: two basements compensating for the uneven ground on the west and the north, for the "offices of household and mouth" and for secretariat offices. A

View of the Royal Palace from Calle Nueva. Fernando Brambilla.

View of the river with part of Madrid and the Royal Palace. Fernando Brambilla.

Fachada Principal del Proyecto de D." Felipe Juvarra, para el Real Palacio de Madrid.

Project for the Royal Palace of Madrid, main façade facing towards the city. Filippo Juvarra, 1735.

lower floor for summer quarters of the Royal Family, and a main floor for the winter quarters. A second floor for the lords and ladies-in-waiting, and finally the rooms in the mezzanines over the lower, principal and second floors, for the servants.

The general ground-plan of the building did not change from the first plan, dated 9 March 1737; it is square, with a single main courtyard, also square, in the centre, surrounded by galleries with arcades. The main rooms are arranged in line along the façades, the antechambers and secondary rooms overlook the courtyard, and between the two ranges of rooms run service corridors. Three small courtyards provide light for the interior rooms at the corners. Something of the spirit of the Alcázar seems to float about the New Palace, since its manifest solidity, the projections or "towers" at the corners, the escarpment below its walls, its elevation and situation, endow it with the air of a fortress.

Between 1738 and 1747, as work was progressing, Sacchetti made some changes in his plan as a result of criticism from the Secretary to the Queen, Marqués Annibale Scotti, and from some of the architects engaged on the project. In 1742, and due to Scotti's influence, he gave greater importance to the staircase, which became double with symmetrical twin flights. Between them he left a hall for social gatherings – what is now the Halberdiers' Room – originally intended for the Chapel, now moved to the north side. In this way, it proved possible to harmonize reminiscences of the Alcázar, Sacchetti's obsession with symmetry, and the urge for ostentation of the Spanish Monarchs, who at that time desired the spaces in the Palace to be of the greatest possible magnificence.

Main façade. Detail.

INHABITANTS OF THE PALACE AND CHANGES IN DECORATION

Interior distribution and decoration are two aspects closely linked in a residence, and they usually change simultaneously, according to the needs and tastes of succeeding generations of occupants. Each reign implies different people and preferences, and moreover, ideas concerning the representation of the Royal Majesty were evolving along with social and political changes: there is a chasm between the significance of the person of the King in the Absolute Monarchy, what it became with Liberalism in the 19th century, and what it now is in a parliamentary democracy.

Fachada del mismo Real Palacio, que mira a la parte de los Jardines.

The plans inside the rear cover show the distribution prevailing during each reign. Ferdinand VI did not think about children, which he did not have, and thus his apartments and those of the Queen proved almost as extensive as required by prevailing contemporary ideas about royal residences. Conversely, Charles III had to have large rooms sub-divided, yet still the Palace always seemed small to him, as to his children. In the eyes of succeeding generations it has come to

Project for the Royal Palace of Madrid, façade facing the gardens. Filippo Juvarra, 1735.

East façade.

Sacchetti

"The Royal Palace is being built with great magnificence, and with even greater expense. Five million pesos have already been spent, and up to four thousand men have worked there at the same time, though now there are no more than one thousand and they are working slowly... Nevertheless, it cannot be denied that this is a superb pile, grandiose and accompanied by everything that could make it beautiful, decorated, comfortable and sufficiently appropriate to the majesty of a Sovereign. To achieve this Sacchetti, from Turin, has given fully of all his talents, and would have given more if he had them; but even so he has not succeeded in pleasing most of those who have eyes. Amongst these there are some who do not approve of the abundance of basements, which if I am not mistaken reach the number of seven; others consider the eleven spans and more of the master walls to be superabundant, since this is not a fortress; yet others do not consider the staircase to be good, but rough and inconvenient; some point their criticism at the courtyards, some at the rooms, the windows and, finally, the swollen costs and the indolence of the workers; and in my view certainly these latter are the most worthy of censure. Even my lackey, who having formerly served an architect now considers himself his disciple, has wished to unleash his miserable critical opinion. I consider it undoubted that, if the magnificent model of the Abbot Juvarra had been put into practice, which model can still be seen at the Retiro, correctors would not have been lacking."
Fr.Norberto CAIMO: *Voyage d'Espagne, fait en l'année 1755 ...* Paris, 1772.

appear larger and larger, even excessive, because ideas have been evolving.

The decoration conceived under Ferdinand VI by Sacchetti, Giaquinto and other artists was of a rather heavy late-Baroque style, but it also was modified with the arrival of Charles III, who brought with him a relatively more sober, classical taste, largely due to the Sicilian Francesco Sabatini, a disciple and son-in-law of Luigi Vanvitelli, architect of the Palace of Caserta. Sabatini directed all aspects of the interior decoration of the Palace, except when the King's will was to entrust it to others (as in the Throne Room or the suite decorated by Gasparini), and he did this by harmonizing the dignity of the design with the richness of the materials. These included the magnificent Spanish marbles of the jambs and socles, a collection of over three-hundred samples being gathered together in the Palace, and the solid mahogany of all the doors, windows and shutters. Sabatini and his team were responsible for producing the designs of the stuccoes, the furniture and the ornamental bronzes (which for the most part have disappeared), and these were executed by a series of Italian and French masters chosen and recruited by him. During the period of almost forty years of his activity at the Palace, from 1760 to 1797, his taste and that of his patrons evolved from an attachment to the Rococo towards the forms of classicism.

Together with Sabatini, the artist whose influence was most profound on the decoration of the New Palace was the painter Anton Raphael Mengs. This was not only because he produced several of his masterpieces here, but also because the high esteem in which he was held by the King converted him into an artistic dictator, who in order to decorate the remaining ceilings freely chose young Spanish painters and imprinted his personal style on them: Francisco Bayeu and Mariano Salvador Maella were the most prominent, displacing the disciples of Corrado Giaquinto who had been omnipotent in the Palace under Ferdinand VI, and had created frescoes of great beauty.

Under Charles III and Charles IV a fundamental element in the decoration were the pictures that entirely covered the walls from the frieze or socle to the cornice: visitors were perplexed at the combination of such an accumulation of masterpieces and the sumptuous decoration of the Palace. In some rooms tapestries would replace the paintings during the wintertime. However, early in the 19th century tastes changed: at the most, one single picture on a wall was enough, on top of the silk hangings or of the wallpapers that began to be used by then. Thus, Ferdinand VII removed the great majority of the masterpieces that later he brought together in the *Royal Painting Gallery*, nowadays the *Prado Museum*.

The appearance of the State Rooms is also decidedly "Ferdinand VII" in style due to other essential features of the furnishings. Charles IV had a passion for French furniture and decorative objects, so that the Royal Collections conserve splendid pieces from that period. This taste was continued by his son Ferdinand VII, who made massive purchases

of Parisian bronze objects mainly between 1818 and 1830: clocks, candelabra and chandeliers. Despite their beauty, they are so numerous that it is not possible to offer an extensive description of each one: when no more details are given, they may be assumed to be in the style of Ferdinand VII and from Paris. The effect of rich "Empire-style" profusion that they then produced must have been tremendous, as they were then concentrated in the western half of the Palace, much more so than nowadays when they are dispersed throughout the residence.

The changes in decoration under Isabel II, though important in the eastern half of the building, and particularly in her private rooms, are insignificant compared to those of both her father and her son, Alfonso XII. The Restoration brought with it a desire to modernise the Madrid Palace according to the standards of Victorian royal residences, within the taste of the late 19th-century conservative bourgeoisie for dark, multicoloured interiors. Work was directed by the architect José Segundo de Lema, and consisted in preparing and decorating a room and other facilities where balls and gala dinners could be held, a

North façade of the Palace, with dome of the Royal Chapel, from the Sabatini Gardens.

Gilded and engraved bronze chandelier. French, 19th century.

Audiences and Visits during the *Ancien Régime*

"His Majesty grants audiences on certain days of the week. Those who wish to have the honour of kissing his hand, to talk with him on any matter or present him with a request, obtain this permission by directing themselves with a written note to the Captain of the Life Guards, in the morning before nine o'clock, who if appropriate will indicate the time for this to be done. To speak with the Infantes, the same steps must be followed ..."

"The riches and beauties contained in this Palace are innumerable... The Keeper or Head Chamberlain who lives in the Palace itself allows all these curiosities to be seen when Their Majesties are absent."

Paseo por Madrid, o Guía del Forastero en la Corte. Madrid, 1815.

The "King's Tower" with the statue of Montezuma, on the main façade of the Palace.

billiard room, a smoking room, and the laying of parquet in many of the private rooms and State Rooms, into which furnishings in the style of the period were also introduced. For this purpose, some important decorative features and frescoes by Mengs were sacrificed. The 20th century has been marked by great restoration schemes carried out after the Spanish Civil War of 1936-1939, and in recent years.

THE VISIT

THE PARADE GROUND AND MAIN FAÇADE

Access to the Royal Palace from the city has always been by way of Calle Mayor (main street) and so on to the Royal Armoury. This building, which was demolished in 1884 and has given its name to the square existing between the Cathedral of La Almudena and the Palace, was located approximately where the great iron railings and entrance gate now stand.

After passing the railings we reach the *Plaza de Palacio*, also known as the *Plaza de Armas* or Parade Ground because military parades and ceremonies take place here. Since the 16th century, this has been the stage on which the pomp of the Court could be displayed to the people, with the main façade of the royal residence as a backdrop. Sacchetti and Ventura Rodríguez conceived this square with open porticoes to connect the Palace with the auxiliary buildings, but Sabatini gave the space its present character of a *cour d'honneur* in the French manner, enclosed by two prolongations of the royal

Royal Palace. North-west angle.

suites, of which the only one to be finished (in 1783, and its decoration in 1788) was the one on the right side known as the *Saint Giles Wing*. The left-hand wing never progressed beyond the level of the first floor.

The low pavilions forming the sides of the square follow the general lines drawn by Sabatini, but they date from the 19th century and, like the railings, they correspond to the project of Narciso Pascual y Colomer (1847), who during the reign of Isabel II completed the one on the right-hand side; the one on the left was built by his successors between 1883 and 1893. The open arches to the left, overlooking the Palace Park, allow us to understand the fascination of this site. On the other side of the river, the Casa de Campo spreads out until linking up with the Monte de El Pardo, and on clear days it is possible to see the Monastery of El Escorial in the distant mountains. The continuity of all these royal properties was even more pronounced while the Royal Seat of La Florida (also known as La Moncloa) existed; it was created by Charles IV, and occupied all of the present-day Argüelles district, in addition to the Western Park and the University Campus.

The Parade Ground

"... One (of the truly beautiful landscapes that have impressed him) is the view from the terrace of the Royal Palace. You cross the Parade Ground, where every morning the military parade is held, passing under a gallery marking the limit of the Palace and the city on the West, and between the white pillars supporting the arches is framed a whole green valley, and deep, descending in steps like a cascade of garden and woodland to the Manzanares, rising up again on the other side, where the scrubland and woods extend in search of the steep peaks of the mountains. The lines are very noble and the general tone of great interest: it helps one to understand the paintings of Velázquez, his immense distances of a sad green bordering on a dull blue."
René BAZIN: *Terre d'Espagne*. Paris, 1905.

Relief of Spain the Arms Bearer. Giovanni Domenico Olivieri.

The forms of the architecture of the Palace, inspired in Bernini and Juvarra, may be observed in detail on the *main façade*. Above a cushioned base, corresponding to the ground floor and to the first mezzanine, rises a course of giant pilasters and columns articulating the main floor, second mezzanine and second floor. The great cornice is surmounted by a balustrade which conceals the lead roofs.

The building was originally given a highly Baroque plasticity and propagandistic sense by the numerous statues carved by a large team of Spanish artists led by the Italian Gian Domenico Olivieri and by Felipe de Castro (from Galicia), the principal sculptors of Ferdinand VI. The statues placed on the surmounting balustrade represented the Kings of Spain, from the first of the Goths to Ferdinand VI; while at the level of the main floor, on the pedestals at the corners, there were pairs of Suevian Kings, Counts of Castile, Kings of Navarre, Aragón and Portugal, pre-Columbian Emperors and two Patron Saints of Spain. This sculptural exuberance increased still further as work progressed, due to the influence of the learned Benedictine monk Fray Martín Sarmiento, who was entrusted with designing the complex iconographic programme. However, it was abruptly suppressed by Charles III, who ordered the removal of all the statues in order to give the building a more classical air. Only with the modern restoration of the façades, concluded in 1973, the statues seen today were replaced. Among the most noteworthy are, at the corners on the main floor level, those of *Montezuma*, Emperor of Mexico, by Juan Pascual de Mena (left), and the Peruvian *Atahualpa* by Domingo Martínez.

Where Sabatini placed the four Doric columns, which allowed him to give more projection to the balcony, Ferdinand VI ordered the installation of the statues of four Roman Emperors born in Hispania: *Honorius* and *Theodosius*, by Olivieri, and *Trajan* and *Arcadius* by Castro; since 1791 they have been in the main courtyard. Above the balcony, with three large arch-shaped window spaces that were also reduced by Sabatini, the relief of *Spain the Arms Bearer of Spain* is by Olivieri.

On the attic level, the clock was made according to a design by Sabatini in 1761, the year being indicated on one of the two bells. The other bell, from the clock of the old Alcázar, is dated 1637. When the sphere was installed, Sabatini removed the castle in relief, the sculpture of the lion with the two globes and the *Plus Ultra* columns, which with the Zodiac (still surviving to the sides) composed a heraldic emblem of the Crown. Statues of the Kings who built the Palace have been returned to the adjoining pedestals.

THE VESTIBULE AND THE MAIN STAIRCASE

There are five doorways on the façade: through the two side ones vehicles enter the small vestibules and from there continue to the Main Courtyard. The three central doorways lead to the main vestibule or *atrium*, where Tuscan columns of pink Sepúlveda limestone give a certain warmth to the whiteness of the Colmenar stone. Carriages

Main staircase.

arriving here leave their occupants (only Monarchs, Heads of State or Ambassadors) at the foot of the Main Staircase on the right-hand side, opposite which stands the statue of Charles III by the sculptor Pierre Michel.

For the staircase Sacchetti conceived two grandiose twin flights, facing each other, which would have given access to the King's apartments on the right side, and to those of the Queen on the left. The two stairwells which were to have contained them were built according to his plan, and today they are respectively the Staircase and the Hall of Columns.

However, Charles III did not like either the form Sacchetti had given to the flights of steps or the layout of the antechambers through which his apartments and those of the Queen were approached, and recalling the staircase of the great Palace of Caserta created in Naples by Vanvitelli, he instructed Sabatini to build a similar single staircase in one of the two stairwells, leaving the other as a ballroom.

Thus, in 1760 Sabatini made the staircase as we see it today, but on the opposite side, to the left. When Charles IV came to the throne

When the Monarchs were leaving the Palace. "On the right hand is the grand staircase: it was lined with battle-axe guards.. In the passage there were two or three military men in undress, and seven or eight old women, who were waiting to present memorials to the king; though they could scarcely be ignorant that the time for asking favours from the King of Spain was passed. After waiting some time, the King and Queen descended the staircase, attended by several officers of state, in full dress: dark blue coats, turned up with crimson, laced with gold ... white smallclothes, and white silk stockings." Michael Joseph QUINN: *A visit to Spain in the latter part of 1822 and the first months of 1823.*

Main staircase. Ceiling fresco painted by Corrado Giaquinto.

The two twin main staircases, the one on the right for the King, and that on the left for the Queen, were an idea of the Marqués Scotti, accepted in 1742. Sacchetti conceived them with great magnificence and scenographic display, but he came up against the criticism of Scotti himself and of his protegé Bonavia, who considered the steps too high. The obsession of making the ascent as comfortable as possible motivated a dispute in the Court that gave rise to various projects, including ones of note by Bonavia, one by the important Roman architects Vanvitelli, Fuga and Salvi, and the alternatives put forward by Sacchetti himself during those years, taking ever more space towards the eastern and western façades.

Bonavia was the first to propose an open stairwell, without intermediate support, an approach in which he was followed by Sacchetti and by the architects of the Roman Academy of San Luca, consulted in 1746. Fuga, Salvi and Vanvitelli, though approving Sacchetti, nevertheless sent a fine design of their own as an appropriate solution, but as the Monarchs did not like it, the polemic had to be solved at the end of 1746 by the Directors of the nascent Academy of Fine Arts of San Fernando. Sacchetti emerged as the winner with his most ambitious project, and in the following years constructed these two spaces which now are the main staircase and the Hall of Columns; but the ramps, the ingenious and theatrical arrangement of which offered nine exits on the main floor, went no further than being constructed in wood, so that the King could see the effect: Charles III did not like it.

in 1789, he ordered the architect to move it to the right-hand side, as it is now, for the reasons of distribution mentioned above. Sabatini reused the same materials and steps. These consist of single pieces of San Agustín marble. They are very low and wide, so that the rise is

Ceiling of main staircase. Religion protected by Spain. Corrado Giaquinto.

extremely gentle, which was important particularly for the sedan chairs used by the ladies to reach the main floor.

The central flight ends in a large landing, where it is advisable to move close to the wall in order to observe the entire space: the lions are by two different sculptors, the stiffer one by Felipe de Castro, and the more flexible one by Robert Michel, gracefully turning its head.

All the ceiling decoration, which was completed in the lifetime of Ferdinand VI, is the work of Corrado Giaquinto, from whose designs G.B. Andreoli made the stuccoes. The frescoes are Giaquinto's second work in the Palace, after those of the Chapel, and as they were painted when Sacchetti's plan for the staircase was still in force, they are designed to be seen from what was then the main exit, now the Camón gallery, where the seated statue of *Charles IV as a Roman Emperor* is now located.

Therefore, it is important to stand close to the wall in order to look at the central allegory representing *Religion protected by Spain*, and then while ascending the second flight one can see the beautiful figures of *Liberality* and *Public Happiness* (to the left), *Magnificence* and *Peace* (to the right), in which contemporaries recognized the characteristic virtues of the reign of Ferdinand VI. *Hercules pulls up the Pillars of Gibraltar before Neptune* in the Camón gallery, above the entrance intended by Sacchetti to lead to the King's apartments, and *The Triumph of Spain over Saracen Power* above the doorway to the Halberdiers' Room, along with other small medallions, complete the pictorial decoration.

Here, two anecdotes must inevitably come to mind. One concerns Napoleon, who on his visit to Madrid stopped on the landing, and turning to the new King Joseph exclaimed, "Brother, you are to have a house much better than mine". The other is the celebrated "Battle on the Palace Staircase", the attempted kidnapping of the child Queen Isabel II by General Diego de León and his soldiers, who were opposed by the Halberdiers, under the orders of Colonel Dulce (1841).

At the top of the staircase there are two other important sculptural portraits of Spanish Monarchs of the Bourbon Dynasty, brought here from the Palace of La Granja: Philip V and his second wife Isabella Farnese, by René Frémin, who also designed the splendid marble and bronze pedestals.

Project for the main staircases.
G.B.Sacchetti, 1745. A.G.P.

Isabella Farnese. René Frémin.

APARTMENTS OF KING CHARLES III

Halberdiers' Room

Sacchetti envisaged this as a hall for dances and festivities, with several galleries at the level of the windows where musicians could be placed. However, Charles III assigned it as a Guard Room, and consequently Sabatini decorated it in the simplest possible manner with Tuscan pilasters, instead of the rich ornamentation it would otherwise have received. Also dating from 1760 is the floor of Colmenar stone and red stone from El Molar; the flagstones were originally intended to pave the gallery surrounding the courtyard on this storey; the floor of the *Saleta* is similar, but is not seen as it is covered by the carpet.

This noble simplicity did not prevent rich pictorial embellishment in the frescoes, where G.B. Tiepolo produced one of his masterpieces, *Venus charging Vulcan to forge the arms of Aeneas*, a topic inspired in a passage from Virgil's Aeneid and chosen for the military function of the room, though it does seem also to allude to Charles III as a warrior hero, and to his mother Queen Isabella Farnese as the promoter of his Italian conquests.

Until the twentieth century the furnishings of this room were very simple, being limited to benches and other objects for the Halberdiers' use, but nowadays it is decorated with important pieces.

On both sides of the fireplace, four of the eight console tables of mahogany and gilded bronze, made in 1791 following a design by

The Guard.

"The Court in Spain made use of an absolutely extraordinary etiquette and grandeur... The service of the Life Guards consisted, as in all the countries where it then existed, such as France, Naples and Spain, in mounting guard inside the Royal Palaces, and in accompanying the Sovereign, on foot or on horseback, wherever he went. At that time the Spanish Royal Family required a considerable suite of attendants... The King used to go out very frequently, going every day for long carriage rides with escort, and spending part of the afternoon at the small palace of El Pardo, close to Madrid. For all this escorts were necessary, and he had them whatever the weather."
Baron de NERVO: *Souvenirs de ma vie...* Paris, 1871.

Ceiling fresco in Halberdiers' Room: Venus charging Vulcan to forge the arms of Aeneas. Giambattista Tiepolo.

Philip V. René Frémin.

Francesco Sabatini for the Dining Room or *Saleta* of Charles IV, in this same Palace. On them are French clocks and two models, in bronze and hard stones, of the Fountain of the Four Rivers created by Bernini in the Piazza Navona of Rome. The pictures above are two fine 18th-century copies of *Sibyls* painted by Raphael in the *Stanza della*

Ceiling fresco in Hall of Columns: The Sun before whose appearance all the forces of Nature are joyful and animated. Corrado Giaquinto.

"At the foot of the stairs I shall leave all my spleen, and prepare myself with unfeigned satisfaction to describe to you the beauty and grandeur of the upper apartments. I know no palace in Europe fitted up with so much true royal magnificence."
Henry SWINBURNE: *Travels through Spain in the years 1775 and 1776...* London, 1779.

Halberdiers' Room, detail of a mahogany and bronze console table designed by Francesco Sabatini, 1791.

Segnatura of the Vatican Palace, and two *landscapes with mythological scenes* by B.M. Agüero (late 17th century).

On the courtyard side there are two further console tables from the early 19th century, in carved and gilded wood, though the tops are of marble and painted plaster (Italian, 17th century). On them stand a beautiful model of a *round temple* with columns (late 18th century), from the Buen Retiro, and another in bronze of Trajan's column.

The two paintings by Luca Giordano (completed by Solimena) portraying *Passages from the Life of Solomon*, with others on the same subject and by the same artist, served as models for the tapestries of the King's apartments in this New Palace, woven at the Royal Tapestry Factory under the direction of Corrado Giaquinto. From the same manufacture are the hanging with the royal coat-of-arms above the fireplace, and the covers for benches in the Chapel, all from the 18th century.

Hall of Columns

This Hall occupies the stairwell which according to Sacchetti's project would have served as access to the Queen's apartments. Its walls are in all details similar to those of the staircase eventually made by Sabatini. The ceiling is different as it was decorated in the time of Charles III, who had the main staircase installed here, on the opposite side to its present position. The stuccoes were designed by Sabatini, and made by Bernardino Rusca in 1761, at the same time as those of

Hall of Columns.

The Washing of the Feet of Maundy Thursday 1875, the 27th March: the first of Alfonso XII. "Some time passed before the multitude came out of the Chapel where the religious service had been held... We entered the Hall of Columns which we found already packed with spectators, more than eight hundred of whom were ladies, all standing around, some on the benches, line upon line, hardly leaving a tiny space for the actors in this drama. In the centre of this space the twelve poor men or "apostles" were sitting on a bench, all with their feet well prepared, bare to the knee and washed as thoroughly as possible with water and soap.

The King, in gala uniform and with a towel around his waist, arrived in procession, followed by Cardinal Moreno... and behind and around them a large number of grandees and marshals... The procession made a halt in the little space in front of the twelve seated men. The Cardinal stepped forward and, helped by a grandee who was carrying a jug and basin, scattered a few drops of perfumed water on each of the line of bare feet. Behind him, the King, kneeling before each foot, rubbed it slightly with the towel, and stooped as though to kiss it, though without doing so.

The ceremony did not last more than ten minutes."

Antonio C.N. GALLENGA: *Iberian Reminiscences. Fifteen years' travelling impressions of Spain and Portugal*. London, 1883.

the Halberdiers' Room; the four medallions in bas-relief depict the *Four Elements*. Between 1762 and the beginning of 1763, Giaquinto painted the fresco, the effect of which is therefore intended to be seen from the first flight of Sabatini's staircase. It should be viewed from very close to the doorway into the room, and if possible, squatting down. The subject involves an allusion to the King in the form of Apollo as a solar deity, since it represents *The Sun at whose appearance all the forces of Nature become joyful and animated*. Apollo, who advances in his chariot through the ring of the Zodiac, is accompanied by the Hours and preceded by Aurora and the Zephyr.

Discus Thrower. Moulded in bronze from an ancient statue brought from Rome by Velázquez in 1651.

After the Washing of the Feet, the Supper.

"The twelve men stood up; they were paraded with great pomp around the room, and then seated in a row along one side of a long table... Behind this, on a high spacious platform, was the Court. In the centre the Infanta Isabel... The far right of the dais was occupied by the diplomatic corps... The King and his immediate suite were the only waiters at the table. Innumberable dishes were delivered at the door, and passed from hand to hand until reaching such distinguished servants who, standing in line along the table, presented them to the humble guests... The most curious of all, however, were the poor twelve apostles, the only ones seated while everyone else there was standing; tense, bewildered and, ... too diffident to dare to look at, much less touch, the exquisite viands that passed under their surprised noses and disappeared to leave room for other even rarer delicacies... The farse... lasted close to an hour, after which the fanfare gave the signal to leave. The King and his suite departed in ceremonial order; the Princess and the Court followed him, and the poor apostles were shown the way to the kitchens, where they were given a more substantial meal, after which each of them could feel happy, with his basket of victuals for his family, and a hundred *reales* in his pocket."

Antonio C.N. GALLENGA: *Iberian Reminiscences. Fifteen years' travelling impressions of Spain and Portugal.* London, 1883.

Lower down, the seasons of the year and the elements are symbolized by Ceres, Bacchus, Venus, Vulcan, Diana, Pan and Galatea .

Also by Giaquinto, and his last work in the Palace, is *The Majesty of the Crown of Spain*, above the doorway. When it was painted this space was the staircase, and this image warned visitors that they were entering the royal apartments.

From the time when Charles IV moved the ballroom here, this became the setting for Court banquets and functions that were not

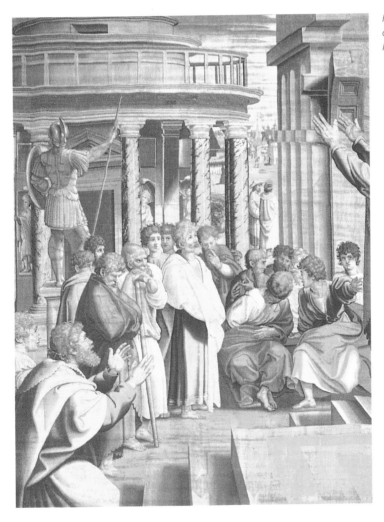

Hall of Columns. Tapestry of The Acts of the Apostles, from cartoons by Raphael of Urbino. Detail.

Planet. Jonghellinck.

simply for amusement, but also ceremonial. For instance, on Maundy Thursday the King washed the feet and served the supper of twelve poor people, who symbolized the Apostles, the entire Court being present at the scene. The Washing of the Feet, a pious custom carried out by other European monarchs besides the Spanish one – and still by the Pope today – continued to take place until the reign of Alfonso XIII. Precisely the tapestries that cover the arches illustrate *The Acts of the Apostles*, and they were woven in Brussels at

View of fresco painting on ceiling of Throne Room: Grandeur and Power of the Spanish Monarchy. Giovanni Battista Tiepolo.

The ceremonial order of the State Apartments of the Palace was governed by etiquette: each room was intended for a specific purpose and access was gradually more restricted. The embryo of this system of distribution, which goes back to the early 16th century, is a nucleus of two rooms: the *sala*, for receiving, and the *cámara* (chamber) for sleeping. By introducing other preliminary and intermediate rooms, the sequence of the King's Apartments arose: Anteroom - *Sala* - *Saleta* - Antechamber - Chamber - small rooms or cabinets. The same order governed the apartments of the other royal personages, but with decreasing amplitude according to the rank of each.

"All the royal family dine publicly in separate rooms; and it is the *etiquette* to visit each apartment whilst they are at dinner; a most tiresome employ for those who are obliged to be there, and it would be thought particular, if the foreign ambassadors were not constantly to attend: Don Luis, the King's brother, who is the lowest in rank is first visited ... the next in turn, is the Infanta Doña Maria [Josefa], who seemed to be a very inoffensive little woman. Then to the two Infantes, Don Gabriel and Don Antonio... Thence to the prince and princess of Asturias, the latter is of the house of Parma, and seems to be very affable."
William DALRYMPLE: *Travels through Spain and Portugal in 1774...* London, 1777.

the beginning of the 17th century from the cartoons painted by Raphael for the famous tapestries now in the Vatican. Three of the bronze sculptures are also Flemish, forming part of the series of the *Seven Planets* cast by Jonghellink around 1570. The fourth statue is a bronze copy of the *Discus Thrower*, commissioned in Rome by Velázquez in 1651. The busts of *Emperors* in porphyry and marble are also Italian, from different periods.

The large sculpture of *The Emperor Charles V dominating the Fury* is a nineteenth-century copy by the Parisian bronzesmith Barbedienne (1878), of Leone Leoni's original work in the Prado Museum. Its placing here in 1879, on a neo-Plateresque pedestal, was intended to evoke the glories of the Spanish branch of the Habsburgs, linking them with those of the Bourbons, and in this sense it should be understood as part of the reorganization of the lay-out and decoration of the Palace by Alfonso XII, who also created a room specifically intended for balls and gala banquets. For this reason, the Hall of Columns has since then been used only for the most formal events, of a ritual nature like the Washing of the Feet, or mournful such as the lying-in-state of the mortal remains of Queen Mercedes, or of a political nature like the signing of the Treaty by which Spain joined the European Community in 1985: for this act the monumental *table of the sphinxes* was used (its design is attributed to Percier and Fontaine, and its bronzes to Thomire; the top contains a varied sampler of mainly non-Spanish marbles). This table was purchased by Charles IV from the widow of the supplier Godon.

Throne Room. Detail of west end, with fresco paintings by G.B. Tiepolo and stuccowork by Robert Michel.

"However, to our great satisfaction, we gain admission to the whole of the State apartments, and their exceeding beauty and richness of decoration, together with the costly display of rare ornaments and furniture, amply gratify our curiosity and desire."
John Benjamin STONE: *A tour with Cook through Spain... as seen and enjoyed in a summer holiday.* London, 1873.

However, the bronze chandeliers (also Parisian, c.1846) correspond to the period when this Hall was most frequently used for festivities and balls, the reign of Queen Isabel II.

From here one continued to the anteroom (*Saleta* of Charles III), in accordance with the ceremonial route in force from the time of Charles IV onwards, but nowadays the aim as far as possible is to follow the order of the King's apartments as they were in the time of Charles III, and therefore a secondary door is used to enter the Throne Room.

The Throne Room

The Throne Room (also known as the Audience Room of the King's apartments, or the Hall of Kingdoms, or of Ambassadors) retains its entire decoration as planned and executed during the reign of Charles III, since it was totally finished by 1772. A recent restoration has returned all its splendour to this magnificent chamber, by cleaning the fresco and replacing the original velvet wall-covering with new material, transferring the original embroidery to the latter.

Here all the Sovereign's ceremonial audiences used to take place, including the last of all, as it was in this room that, according to etiquette, the mortal remains of the King lay in state prior to their removal to the Pantheon of San Lorenzo el Real. Then the tables, decorative mirrors and canopy were removed, and the draperies were changed.

Although Sacchetti had planned to cover all the walls of this gallery with marble which would have framed the mirrors and bas-reliefs, nothing of this was done before the arrival of Charles III. The King

Throne Room. Detail of the embroidery and gilded carving made in Naples following designs by G. Battista Natale.

Throne Room. Detail of fresco. Giovanni Battista Tiepolo.

Audience of the 8th December 1783, festivity of the Immaculate Conception, patron of the Order of Charles III; the King returns from the ceremony in the Chapel.

"We were almost the first to reach the Ambassadors' Hall. The pages had formed a group around the brazier; they were dressed in blue and wore stockings in an orange tone of red... Little by little a veritable multitude arrived and filled the entire room. One might say that it is impossible to bring together such a strange collection of personages, even seeking them here and there. My attention was struck by some Staff officers with their canes, a large number of gentlemen of all kinds, and two Capuchins. Regarding the room, its walls are hung with magnificent crimson velvet, with bulky gold decoration and embroidery. On the ceilings there are some very fine figures, with typically Spanish features. The mirrors are of extraordinary height and width. In cages there were parrots and other birds whose plumage had beautiful colours. The King, the Prince and the two Infantes passed through the room in a solemn procession, coming from the Chapel. They wore large white cloaks with blue decorations (of the Order of Charles III), as did the grandees and high-ranking courtiers who preceded and followed them."

Daniel Gotthilf MOLDENHAWER: *Relación de su viaje a España en 1782-1783,* published by Emile Gigas. Paris, 1927.

decided that the decoration of this room should be directed by his man of confidence in matters of good taste, Count Gazzola, who commissioned the designs for the furnishings from the Piacenza architect Giovanni Battista Natale. Apparently, the choice of the painter and of the sculptor who decorated the vault may also be attributed to Gazzola.

The magnificent effect of this union between painting, sculpture and decorative design reaches its apogee in the corners of the ceiling and the panels over the doors. The Court sculptor Robert Michel created the ornamental stuccoes above the doorways and the cornice, with a brightness and fresh inventiveness comparable to those displayed by the great Tiepolo on the ceiling, his last masterpiece, which has always been the object of well-deserved praise even amongst his own contemporaries.

The Grandeur and Power of the Spanish Monarchy is here expressed through a large number of allegorical and allusive figures scattered over a background of open sky. When Tiepolo painted the fresco, access to the room was from the present Official *Saleta*, at that time the antechamber to the King's apartments (the ceiling of the *Saleta* was also painted by Tiepolo, with a similar subject), and so the composition has to be understood by entering from that side. Advancing from the door to approximately half-way along the room, the central group can be seen well: this is the *Spanish Monarchy*, the throne of which is set on a

Throne Room.

The Throne Room.

"The largest and most magnificent room in the Palace due to the superb mirrors and the rich furnishings with which it is decorated... Tiepolo had a great deal of imagination and painted with both warmth and ease..."
Jean François PEYRON: *Nouveau voyage en Espagne fait en 1777 et 1778, & Essais sur l'Espagne.*

Throne Room. Prudence, attributed to Foggini.

large globe flanked by the statues of Apollo and Minerva, surrounded by the Science of Government, Peace and Justice (near which the flying figure of Virtue is portrayed) and by Abundance and Mercy. The canopy to the throne of the Monarchy is formed by a ring of clouds surrounded

Throne Room. Detail of fresco, opposite throne: The Olympian Gods and figures representing the American Provinces of the Spanish Crown. Giovanni Battista Tiepolo.

"I had before seen all the palaces of the kings of England, France, Sardinia, Naples, Prussia, and Portugal; those of the pope, the emperor, and of several German princes; and I give the preference to this; but it may possibly be equalled by the palace which the king of Naples is now building at Caserta, and of which I saw part in 1769". Richard TWISS: *Travels through Portugal and Spain in 1772 and 1773*. London 1775.

Mars. Jonghellinck.

by geniuses, one of whom holds the Royal Crown in the very centre of the vault. Behind this entire section of the composition, and appropriately placed adjacent to the entrance to the King's apartments, is a pyramid or monument in honour of Charles III, with the figures of Magnanimity, Glory, Affability and Counsel. Close by are those of the three theological virtues, in addition to Prudence, Fortitude and Victory. Finally, the Fine Arts are "depicted in one of the corners of the ceiling, showing with their attributes that they are to perpetuate the glories of the great Prince who has been their restorer".

This glorification of the Monarchy and of the Sovereign constitutes the main part of the allegory: the other half of the vault of heaven represented by the composition, the farthest from the entrance door, is inhabited by the Olympian gods. Prominent amongst them is Mercury, who as the ambassador of the gods before the Monarchy, seems to be announcing Peace on behalf of Jupiter. Apollo, sun god and protector of the Arts, is exactly over the King's throne. To the left stands Mars expelling Crime and the Furies, and opposite the throne, in a dominant position, is Neptune.

In the lowest part of the fresco, above the cornice, a numerous and varied series of characters is portrayed, possibly the most appealing part of this composition. They represent the kingdoms of the Iberian Peninsula and the countries at that time subject to the Crown of Spain: on the entrance side, Andalusia, Catalonia, Aragón, Castile and Granada; on the opposite side, the East Indies, in addition to the Basque Country, Cantabria, Asturias and Murcia; and on the

Throne Room. Corner with furnishings made in Naples from designs by G.Battista Natale.

The Public Audience.
"On entering the Parade Ground, the carriage of the Nuncio or Ambassador will pass between the rows of the parade or guard, which, having formed previously, will do the regulation honours, playing the Royal March... The Nuncio or Ambassador will alight at the foot of the main staircase *(as is only the case with royal personages).* Other persons ... will alight at the side doors of the Royal Palace, but inside it. On the main staircase will be lined up the companies of Royal Guard Halberdiers led by their band, to do the corresponding honours; also ... the Gentlemen-in-Waiting of the week and the Gentlemen of household and mouth... the Presenter of Ambassadors accompanies him to the Audience Room, where he is received by the Sovereign, seated on the throne, with the Princes and Princesses on his right and the Ministers and great officers of the Palace on his left: on both sides of the room the foreign Ministers and persons of the Court are situated. The Ambassador, accompanied by his Secretaries and Attachés, approaches the throne, and makes a bow three times; the Prince removes his hat in greeting, and indicates to the Ambassador the chair he should occupy in front of the throne; the Ambassador sits, and putting on his hat, delivers a solemn speech... The Sovereign immediately replies, and thus the audience terminates."
Guía Palaciana, Nº 19. Madrid, 1899.

long side over the balconies, starting from the farthest end, America with Christopher Columbus and several figures alluding to the Discovery, and then León, Galicia, Valencia and Extremadura. It is no simple matter to identify them, since Tiepolo has envisaged them with a great deal of artistic licence, in a tone of fantastic exoticism and with

Throne dais in the Throne Room. Carpet from reign of Ferdinand VII, with Both Worlds, an 18th-century emblem of the territorial extension of the old Spanish Monarchy. Giovanni Battista Tiepolo.

Besamanos.

"As for Court ceremonials, there cannot be the slightest doubt that they are not lacking. The one that takes place with the greatest frequency is the irritating farce of eating under the vigilant gaze of the public. That of the *besamanos*, or presentation of respects, is only held on certain feast days. It is performed by parading in Indian file (to borrow a military expression), and also with Indian rapidity. However, it lasts sufficiently long to test, and even exhaust, the patience of some of the younger members of the Royal Family ...

This formal ceremony takes place in front of the Royal Family before they eat separately, not in a group, as all the royal personages have their own dining rooms. The file of persons to be presented, diplomats, military men and civil servants, passes in an orderly manner, in accordance with their rank and in the corresponding dress, to take their places in a line, flowing through the Palace from one apartment to another; each person, bending a knee, kisses the hand of the royal personage before whom he is being presented, and the ceremony concludes when the line comes to an end."
Maurice KEATING: *Travels through France and Spain to Morocco* (1785). London, 1817.

no preoccupation for rigour, though with grace and picturesque flair both in the whole and in the details: these include, just above the throne, a pageboy trying to catch a macaw, directly in front of the group representing America.

The remaining decoration, including the console tables, mirrors, canopy, throne and draperies, are to be understood as a whole conceived by Gazzola and the Italian artists selected by him, everything being brought from Italy, an indication of the devotion felt by Charles III for Neapolitan formulas.

Throne Room. Top of a mirror.

"The reception rooms are large, well-proportioned and beautifully adorned... the grandeur of this palace resides in the sequence of fine, well-decorated apartments." George Downing WHITTINGTON: *Travels through Spain and part of Portugal*. London, 1808.

The velvet was woven expressly in Genoa, thereby achieving exceptional quality, and afterwards it was sent to Naples for embroidery with gilded silver thread by the needleworker of that Court, Andrea Cotardi (or Gottard). From the various designs invited from Madrid, Paris and Naples, those selected were the ones submitted by Giovanni Battista Natale, like Gazzola a native of Piacenza, who was also responsible for designing the console tables and mirrors made by the woodcarver Gennaro di Fiore. Between the summer of 1765 and November of the following year, all the decorative elements for this Royal Audience Chamber were made ready, though they did not occupy their intended places until 1772.

Throne Room. Bronze lions. Matteo Bonicelli, 1651.

The decorative scheme designed by Natale is a key work of Italian Rococo fantasy. The characteristic themes of the late Baroque represented by Natale in the decorative carving of the twelve mirrors and matching tables, are in perfect accord with the magnificent exoticism of Tiepolo, vaguely alluding to the extensive dominions of the Spanish Monarchy: the four parts of the world, the four seasons of the year (or the four periods of life), and the four elements. The whole scheme thus consists of generous rhetorical praise for the power that has there its seat.

The bronze sculptures were also placed in the Throne Room at that time, but all are of an earlier date. The four cardinal virtues along the wall on the throne side are usually attributed to René Frémin, as having been made for the altarpiece of the Collegiate Church at La Granja, but they have also been attributed to Foggini.

"The Muses". Detail of fresco in Saleta of Charles III, Apotheosis of Trajan. Anton Raphael Mengs.

"The room where the throne is situated, and the one known as *Hall of Kingdoms*, is worthy of admiration even after seeing the Gallery of Versailles. On the ceiling a Venetian called Tiepolo has painted *al fresco* the diverse costumes of the vast Spanish Monarchy, a type of decoration that can only correspond to the Palace of the Sovereign of the Spains ... The mirrors, which are of a size assuredly unique in Europe, have been manufactured at San Ildefonso..."
Jean François BOURGOING: *Nouveau voyage en Espagne...* Paris, 1788.

"In my opinion it is the most magnificent room in all Europe... the Throne represents grandeur in a perfect manner."
John Benjamin STONE: *A tour with Cook through Spain... as seen and enjoyed in a summer holiday.* London, 1873.

Mercury, Jupiter, Saturn and *Mars*, with three more situated in the Hall of Columns, make up the series of the *Seven Planets* by Jonghellinck; the other two, a *Satyr* and *Germanicus*, are moulded from classical statues commissioned by Velázquez and made in Rome. Also from Rome, and dating from 1651, are the bronze lions by Matteo Bonicelli, ordered by Velázquez to decorate the Hall of Mirrors in the Alcázar.

The two chandeliers of rock crystal and silver were bought in 1780 from the Venetian Ambassador, Francesco Pesaro, on the warm recommendation of Sabatini. It is paradoxical that such items came to complete this Rococo setting when their style was already outmoded, and only ten years before, on the instructions of Charles IV, Sabatini began to plan a new scheme of decoration for this room, radically architectural and classical, using marble and bronze with Corinthian pilasters, but this project was never carried out.

Charles IV must, however, be credited with the acquisition of three of the four splendid clocks with complex time and musical mechanisms: to the right of the canopy, a large grandfather clock with an ebony and bronze case in the Louis XVI style, made by Ferdinand Berthoud in Paris around 1780; on the left, another also of ebony and bronze in the English Rococo style, by John Ellicot. Opposite, a monumental table clock by Furet and Godon, of white marble and bronze, representing Music and Astronomy. Of the same materials and taste (Louis XVI, around 1780), on the neighbouring console table is another piece by "Godon clockmaker and machinist of HCM". Ferdinand VII respected the decoration of his grandfather's time, but added the large carpet woven at the Royal Factory of Madrid. To his reign and that of his father correspond the Empire-style candelabra on the console tables.

Saleta of Charles III.
"Fame proclaiming the Name of Trajan". Detail of the fresco, Apotheosis of Trajan. Anton Raphael Mengs.

Finally, the feature giving its name to the room: the *Throne*. The original chair, of which the two seen here are faithful copies, is in the Palace of La Granja and bears the portrait of Charles III in the relief surmounting the back. Alfonso XII ordered a copy to be made of the chair, having his own profile placed in the medallion. Alfonso XIII followed suit, adding another one with Queen Victoria Eugenia's portrait in order to place them together. Similarly, the present ones carry the images of Their Majesties King Juan Carlos and Queen Sofia.

Saleta of Charles III

This was the room where the King used to take his luncheon and where ordinary audiences were granted. At that time, its walls were covered during the winter with tapestries from the series of the *History of David, Solomon and Absalom*, woven at the Royal Tapestry Factory, while during the summer eight large equestrian portraits were hung here, major works of Rubens and Velázquez now in the Prado Museum. But since the reign of Ferdinand VII, the pictures displayed here are four works by Giordano, two on the *Life of*

The King's Luncheon.

"His Majesty lunches alone in the room in his Apartments reserved for this purpose, and it is there, at table, that the Ministers present him with their respects. The King had scarcely started to eat, when they greeted him and withdrew, to go to the Apartments of the Prince, who was also taking luncheon. Afterwards, they returned to the King's presence, just before his table was removed. Sometimes they accompany him to his study, remaining there with him for a quarter of an hour, and it is then that the King converses with some of them.

One gentleman places the dishes on the King's table as they are passed to him; then it is the pages who carry them. The one who presents the King with water or wine, kneels when the King begins to drink. During the meal the Nuncio remains standing a few steps in front of the table, and the King talks almost exclusively with him. When the King has finished eating, the Patriarch, who is a prelate, and therefore is dressed in the same manner as the Nuncio and the Confessor, says the prayer of thanksgiving that hardly lasts more than two or three seconds. The King crosses himself, cleans his mouth and hands, and enters his Apartments.

... I also saw the Prince during his luncheon. He eats alone with the Princess, who is served by two ladies. Like the Prince, she speaks from time to time with one or other of the Ambassadors.

... After taking luncheon, the King immediately changed his clothes and went hunting."

Daniel Gotthilf MOLDENHAWER: *Relación de su viaje a España en 1782-1783*, published by Emile Gigas. Paris, 1927.

Solomon, and the other two showing scenes from Roman history, *Quintus Curtius throwing himself into the Chasm* and the *Death of Seneca*.

On the ceiling is an outstanding fresco by A.R. Mengs, *The Apotheosis of Trajan* (1774). This Roman Emperor, who was born in Hispania and is used here as the *alter ego* of Charles III, is portrayed on the side opposite the entrance, seated on his throne, wearing the imperial purple and surrounded by Minerva, Hercules and Glory, who is crowning him. Different allegories of Victory and her virtues are grouped on the long sides, while at the opposite end are a number of figures including the nine Muses and the Arts, around the temple of Apollo. It is a veritable discourse on the enlightened Monarch's virtues, his protection of the Arts, and so on.

The stucco designs of Sabatini were executed by Andreoli between 1761 and 1763. Also from the reign of Charles III are all the marble features and (although the present ones had not yet been installed here) the four console tables with their corresponding mirrors. From Paris are the two large chandeliers in the style of Ferdinand VII, and the circular couch with bronzes by Thomire and the initials of Isabel II on the upholstery: it dates from 1846, but was not placed here until the end of the 19th century, when the long couches were also installed at the ends. The stools are from the same period. The carpet, from the Royal Factory, is dated 1880; from this period also were the silk wall-hangings, but due to their poor condition they were copied and replaced in 1994.

After Charles IV ordered the main staircase to be moved to its current location, this *Saleta*, which formerly was entered directly from the Hall of Columns, became the first room of the King's apartments, which extended eastwards in the opposite order to that prevailing in the time of Charles III, when it was occupied by the Prince of Asturias.

Antechamber of Charles III

The Antechamber or "Conversation Room" was where the King dined, and as such it appears (though with an "invented" ceiling) in the painting by Paret of *Charles III dining before his Court*. The tapestries that then decorated it were those of the *History of Joseph*, made at the Royal Factory from cartoons painted in 1770 by José del Castillo, under the direction of Giaquinto. During the summer masterpieces by Titian, Van Dyck and Velázquez, including *The Meninas*, used to hang here. Originally intended for this room were the magnificent console tables of hard-stones and bronze, masterpieces of the Royal Factory of the Buen Retiro, and nowadays in the Prado Museum.

The marble decoration from the reign of Charles III has survived, and from the same period is the very good fireplace which, unusually, still retains its bronzes. However, painting, both of the ceiling and on canvas, is the absolute protagonist of this room.

The fresco by Anton Raphael Mengs depicts *The Apotheosis of Hercules*. The hero, traditionally used in Spain as the personification or emblem of the King, is welcomed among the gods on Mount Olympus as a reward for his great feats: the aim is to praise Charles III as an

Antechamber of Charles III.

illustrious military and political figure, as well as patron of the Arts, to which the beautiful group of Apollo and the Muses above the entrance door refers. The restrained decorative stuccoes, made by Bernardino Rusca, were also designed by the painter and not by Sabatini. The latter yielded to his friend Mengs after confronting Giaquinto, who was initially to have decorated this ceiling. The incident with his two rivals, who were favoured by the King, led the painter of Ferdinand VI to decide to leave Spain, by now old and infirm. The four oval reliefs in the corners are by Felipe de Castro.

The canvases, masterpieces by Goya, are two pairs of portraits of *Charles IV* and his wife Queen *María Luisa of Parma*: one set is more formal, showing the King wearing the uniform of Colonel of the Life Guards and the Queen in Court dress, while the other is more casual, with the King wearing hunting attire and the Queen dressed as a

Charles IV. Francisco de Goya.

The King's Dinner.
"At dinner the pages bring in the
different dishes and present them to
one of the Gentlemen of the
Chamber on duty that day; he places
them on the table; another
gentleman remains standing near the
King to serve him wine and water,
which he first tastes and then
presents kneeling; the Patriarch
attends to give the blessing, and also,
further away, are the Inquisitor
General on one side, and the Captain
of the Guard on the other. The
Ambassadors form a circle around
and converse with the King for a
moment when they withdraw with
him to the neighbouring room, which
is entered by the door behind his
chair. The rest of the Court forms a
second outer circle. When the King
rises from the table, all those to be
presented to him come forward, and
if the Corregidor of Madrid receives
an appropriate indication he enters
with the Ambassadors into the
Chamber. The King goes out to take
exercise every day of the year, even
in rain or storm, though if in Madrid
he only does so in the afternoon, but
if he is in the country, at one of the
Seats, he goes out morning and
afternoon."
William DALRYMPLE: *Travels through
Spain and Portugal in 1774...*
London, 1777.

Spanish *"maja"*, with a black skirt and mantilla. These are the most
outstanding paintings to be seen today in the Palace, and the first pair
have been in this room since the reign of Ferdinand VII. As a
counterpoint to Goya's works, we have two marble busts of the same
royal couple, by Juan Adán (1797).

Maria Luisa of Parma, dressed as a "Maja". Francisco de Goya.

"Mars and other Olympian gods". Detail of fresco on ceiling of Antechamber of Charles III, Apotheosis of Hercules. Anton Raphael Mengs.

Also from the reign of Charles IV are the console tables and the monumental mahogany and bronze clock in the shape of a small temple, with a flute organ (housed in the base) and alabaster sculptures: the main figure portrays *Chronos supporting the Celestial Sphere*. The design is attributed to J.D. Dugourc. It was the last work

"The number of ceremonial rooms is interminable, and all with their ceilings very well painted. Most of the best paintings that used to adorn their walls are now in the Museum, however. I cannot tell you anything further about the interior, as the Queen is there at present..."
ANONYMOUS: *Spain, Tangier, etc., visited in 1840 and 1841*. By X.Y.Z. London, 1845.

(1799) of the clockmaker Louis Godon, a distinguished supplier of Parisian decorative objects to Charles IV.

Chamber of Charles III, known as the Gasparini Room

The Chamber was where the King dressed and received private audiences. Therefore, we should not be surprised at the excellence with which Charles III wished it to be decorated, entrusting the design of each and every element to his royal painter Matteo Gasparini, whom he had brought with him from Naples. It is logical that the artist's name has served to identify this room of the Palace since the time of Ferdinand VII, inasmuch as the marble floor, the stucco ceiling, the silk wall-hangings embroidered with gold and silver thread, the furniture of precious woods and bronzes, were all entirely designed by Gasparini, who until his death directed this supreme work of the *barochetto*. After his death it was continued under the supervision of his widow and son, and of his successor in the post of "Chamber Decorator", G.B. Ferroni.

Made by Italian craftsmen and German cabinetmakers, this room can claim to be of Madrid only insofar as it was commissioned in this city by one who had previously been King of Naples, and in reality it is an international work, one of the most perfect examples of the European late Baroque. The Rococo decoration based on asymetrical vegetation shines forth in its maximum splendour, heavy with exotic fantasy of Chinese inspiration. One cannot but admire its magnificence, though to find the taste for it and to lose oneself happily amongst its rich arabesques it is necessary to forget Goya and Mengs, escaping into the dream world also suggested by the Throne Room.

The ceremony of "covering" a Grandee of Spain.

"It is held in the Antechamber, like all acts of strict etiquette... while the Grandees to be covered await their turn, accompanied by their sponsors, in the *Saleta*, and the invited covered Grandees and Ladies wait in the Antechamber, the screen giving access to the Chamber is opened, and Her Majesty appears followed by her senior staff, and after the grave Court bow, takes her seat... and addressing the Ladies who are to her right, says: *be seated*, and to the Grandees who are to her left: *be covered*... The person to be favoured with the honour is led in by his sponsor, holding his right hand, while the left is held by the Major-domo for the week. As he enters the Ladies rise and the Grandees take off their hats; the neophyte and his companions, when they are two steps from the door, make the first bow to Her Majesty, in the centre of the room the second, and close to the Royal Person the third. The sponsor and Major-domo withdraw, and the Queen says: *Be covered, and speak*... (at this point there are nuances depending on the category of grandee), then he takes off his hat, genuflects, kisses the Royal hand..."
Guía Palaciana, N° 31. Madrid, 1900.

Chamber of Charles III, or Gasparini Room. Detail.

Chamber of Charles III. Detail of the embroidered fabric. Matteo Gasparini and team.

This decorative scheme is preserved intact, and indeed, more complete than when its creator and the Monarch who commissioned it were able to contemplate it, since such extensive work took many years to complete. As the embroidered wall-hangings were not finished until 1802, fourteen years after the death of Charles III,

Chamber of Charles III. Detail of the furniture in fine woods, bronze and embroidered upholstery designed by Matteo Gasparini.

María Luisa of Parma, in Court dress. Francisco de Goya.

during his reign in wintertime the walls were hung with tapestries made by the Royal Factory, from cartoons by Antonio Gónzalez Velázquez in the style of David Teniers, of whom the King was so fond. In summertime, paintings by Diego Velázquez were hung here, including *Vulcan's Forge*, *The Tapestry Weavers* and *The Tipplers*, in addition to works by Murillo, Ribera and Titian. Since the King greatly admired Mengs, this artist's last work, *The Annunciation*, was also displayed here; it is now in the Royal Chapel.

To Gasparini is also due the design of the case of the small English clock (by Martineau) standing on the console table between the balconies. Much more important, both for its fine case in the Louis XV style and its complex mechanism with music and automatons, is the *shepherd's clock*, built by Jacques Droz in Switzerland and acquired by Ferdinand VI in 1756.

The embroidered wall-hangings were not installed until 1815. Alfonso XII had them restored in 1879, and since then the curtains, which are also embroidered and used to cover the doors and windows, are in storage. In the last great restoration campaign the embroidery was transferred onto a new silk background.

With the exception of the superb set of chairs of fine woods and bronze, none of the furniture corresponds to Gasparini's scheme. From the time of Charles IV are the exellent console tables, with bronzes by Domingo Urquiza and work by the cabinetmakers of the royal workshops, as well as the French candelabra, including outstanding examples of the "Etruscan" taste in porcelain and bronze. The splendid chandelier has the greatest symbolic meaning of the many such pieces commissioned by Ferdinand VII, displaying his monogram and that of his third wife María Josefa Amalia of Saxony. The table

Chamber of Charles III, or Gasparini Room.

Chinoiserie stuccoes. Gennaro de Matteis and others, from designs by Matteo Gasparini.

Detail of a frieze originally in the "Indies-wood Rooms" of Charles III.

corresponds to the period of Isabel II: it was designed and made in Rome by Gerardo Volponi and Guglielmo Chidel, under the direction of Filippo Agricola in 1848.

Three adjoining small rooms which are not visited were the offices of Charles III, the so-called "rooms of woods from the Indies", due to the rich decoration also designed by Gasparini, which subsequently was dismantled and installed in other rooms of the Palace. Ferdinand VII, who also had his study or cabinet in this suite, commissioned the ceiling frescoes by Luis López.

The "Tramcar" of Charles III

This room was given its present layout in 1880, when an attempt was made to improve the flow between the Gasparini Room and the new Gala Dining Room; its name also dates from that time, alluding to its long, narrow shape. Until then there had been two rooms here: one was used only as a passageway, as it is nowadays, being very small but literally covered by pictures during the reigns of Charles III and Charles IV, and overfilled with furniture in that of Isabel II; the other interior room was larger, and served as the Oratory of Charles III, with access from the Chamber. It was designed by Sabatini, the walls being adorned with green Lanjarón marble and gilded bronzes made in 1767-1768 by Urquiza, Vendetti and Beya: the ceiling with stuccoes, was by Bernardino Rusca; over the high altar was a fresco by Mengs, *The Adoration of the Shepherds*. Other similar oratories, designed and built by Sabatini with a similar degree of magnificence, were also dismantled at the end of the 19th century. These spaces, destined for morning and evening devotions, were important in the daily life of the royal personages.

Chamber of Charles III, or Gasparini Room. Detail of the Chinoiserie stuccoes on the ceiling, and of the embroidered wall-hangings.

A free visitor.

"Not a door being closed, I penetrated through the chamber of the throne even into the old king's sleeping-apartment [Charles III]... In this room, as in all the others I passed through, without any exception, stood cages of gilded wire, of different forms and sizes, and in every cage a curious exotic bird, in full song, each trying to outsing his neighbour. Mingled with these warblings was heard at certain intervals the low chime of musical clocks, stealing upon the ear like the tones of harmonic glasses. No other sound broke in any degree the general stillness, except indeed, the almost inaudible footsteps of several aged domestics, in court-dresses of the cut and fashion prevalent in the days of the king's mother, Elizabeth Farnese, gliding along quietly and cautiously to open the cages...
I availed myself of the light reflected from a clear sun-set to examine the pictures, chiefly of a religious cast with which these stately apartments are tapestried, particularly the Madonna del Spasimo... I stood fixed in the contemplation of this holy vision... till the approaching shadows of night had overspread every recess of these vast apartments... The song of the birds had ceased, as well as the soft diapason of the self-played organs; all was hushed, all tranquil".
William BECKFORD: *Italy, with sketches of Spain and Portugal...*(1787). London, 1834.

Now there are two console tables here, dating back to around 1780, the design of which is ascribed to Sabatini; two portraits, *Francis of Portugal* attributed to Ranc, and *James (III) Stuart* attributed to Francisco Trevisani; and a tapestry cartoon, *The Wild-Boar Hunt* by Francisco de Goya. In the restoration campaign of 1991 new fabric was installed on the walls of this room; it was specially made with the ciphers of King Juan Carlos and Queen Sofía.

Hall of Charles III

The first plans for the distribution of the royal apartments designated this as a bedroom, and so it was for Charles III, from 1764 until the 13th of December 1788, when he died here. Nothing remains of the original furniture, which was selected by Sabatini, and included outstanding tapestries, carved and gilded chairs by Chiani and Balce, and the splendid fireplace bronzes of Vendetti. The paintings, on the *Passion of Christ*, were all by Mengs: four above the doorways, and a large *Descent from the Cross* by Mariano Salvador Maella, where now hangs the portrait of Charles III, this Monarch of the Enlightenment being portrayed in the ceremonial habit of the honorary Order that he founded to reward merit; he had named it after himself, placing it under the patronage of the Immaculate Conception of the Virgin, for whom he felt a particular devotion. The present aspect of this room is that of a sanctuary, dedicated to Charles III and to his Order by his grandson Ferdinand VII, as expressed by the Latin inscription on the ceiling: "To Charles III, a deeply religious Monarch, instituting the Spanish Order under the protection of the Immaculate Virgin / To reward virtue and merit / On the very ceiling beneath which he passed on to a better life

Detail of the Allegory of The Institution of the Order of Charles III. Vicente López.

"Peking", 18th-century Chinese fabric used in wall-hangings for the royal bedrooms and sitting rooms in summer.

and to receive a greater heavenly recompense for his virtue and his merit / His grandson Ferdinand VII wished this to be painted in the year 1828". Ferdinand VII, who had also been using this Room as a bedroom when he was Prince of Asturias, turned it into his dressing room after he became King.

The furniture of white and gilded wood is typical of the Ferdinand VII style. The new, elegant neo-classical fireplace in the Ionic order, in white, pink and green marble, seems to be Italian. The blue grogram wall-hangings with superimposed white motifs alluding to the Order, are also in the Ferdinand VII style: stripes, stars, castles, lions and ciphers of Charles III; they are original, except for the blue silk background which has twice been replaced, the first time during the reign of Alfonso XII, and the second during the 1986 restoration.

In addition to the overall effect, the most remarkable aspect of this decorative scheme is the fresco painting on the ceiling, where Vicente López portrayed *The Institution of the Order of Charles III*: the King, in gala uniform and with all the emblems of sovereignty, is kneeling before the Immaculate Virgin. Near the altar are figures representing Religion, Piety, Gratitude, the Spanish Monarchy, Public Happiness and Pleasure. Above the south wall, over the fireplace, are Nobility, Honour, Merit and Virtue; while above the opposite wall is an allegory of the Benefits of Peace, accompanied by "Noble Agriculture" and children throwing weapons into a blazing abyss, where the dragon of Discord is also to be seen, while Evil and Rebellion are fleeing. Over the balconies, History, Time and Fame. The stucco decoration on the cornice is by José Tomás and José Ginés, completing that of the fresco: at the corners, sustained by geniuses are four emblems alluding to the

Hall of Charles III.

"Regarding its interior, it is a world of marvels: everything that could exist of the richest and most varied furnishings of all types, and sumptuous draperies, decorates the rooms and the vast halls with walls that are stuccoed or brilliantly covered with fine porcelain; purple, gold, marble and crystal seem to rival eachother to reflect the light against a thousand different objects and emphasize the wonderful paintings, in which the best masters have succeeded in animating this grandiose residence of the Kings of Spain with the most diverse themes taken from Mythology, from Religion and from History, managing on occasion to produce a full illusion."
MATHIEU, A.: *L'Espagne, lettres d'un Français à un ami.* Madrid, 1887.

Charles III. Mariano Salvador Maella.

King; and in the central section three reliefs on the foundation of the Order and its aims.

Ferdinand VII kept the pictures of Mengs in their original places, and he decorated this dressing room with furniture that is no longer here, since under Alfonso XIII the console tables and the Ferdinand VII mirrors were replaced by the present ones, which are in the Rococo style and therefore earlier. Of the immense profusion of decorative bronze objects that were once here, two extraordinary pieces have been retained in their places: the chandelier in the shape of a fleur-de-lys, heraldic symbol of the Bourbon Dynasty, purchased in Paris around 1825 for this room by order of Ferdinand VII; and the amphora clock (c. 1800), of gilded and blued bronze, with clock and automatons by J.F. De Belle, also from Paris.

Although it was not placed here until the reign of Isabel II (who otherwise fully respected the Ferdinand VII- style decoration of this Room), the sumptuous *Pedestal Table of the Coronation of Charles X* (1825), in bronze and Sèvres porcelain, a gift from the French Monarch to his Spanish counterpart, also dates back to the reign of Ferdinand VII.

Porcelain Room

Encouraged by his wife, who was from Saxony, Charles III had created near Naples the famous Capodimonte Porcelain Factory, workers and materials from which he had brought to Madrid in 1760, setting up the Royal Factory of the Buen Retiro. He wished to have in his Spanish palaces a porcelain room like that of the Portici Palace, and he commenced with the one in Aranjuez. Only when it was

completed, by 1765, was the preparation of another "China Room" begun for the Palace of Madrid, the installation being completed in 1771. The porcelain work is by the same team, directed by Giuseppe Gricci and Cayetano Scheppers, but attention has always been drawn to the drastic change in taste to be observed between the two rooms: as against the Chinese shapes and themes of Aranjuez, directly linked to the Portici room designed by Natale, the one in Madrid adopts classical late-Baroque forms, which, in general, have been less appreciated than the unrestrained Rococo of the other room. The design is close to the taste of Ferroni, but the author is unknown. Names invoked have included the painters Juan Bautista de la Torre and Gennaro Boltri, employees of the Factory. The splendid porcelain and bronze vases also come from the Buen Retiro, but are of a very different taste from that of the walls, since they date from the reign of

Porcelain Room.

Detail of the Porcelain Room.

Yellow Room.

The Art of painting.

"Emulation, it is to be supposed has made them all do their best. In my private opinion *Corrado's* invention is more fanciful and various than that of the rest: but Mengs is by far the best painter, as his invention is not much inferior to *Corrado's,* his design much more correct, and his colouring quite magick. The King thinks him the greatest painter of the age, and as His Majesty has been from his infancy used to live in apartments rich in pictures of the best kind his opinion must certainly carry a great weight, whatever contempt some cyniks may affect for the connoisseurship of a king. Some other of those ceilings are to be ornamented with various carvings gildings and stucco's, and some other still in other manners. But, as I said, every thing is at present in the utmost confusion, as nothing is perfectly finished... But besides the rich furniture destined to each of the royal apartments, some pieces of which are already placed, the King is possessed of an immense collection of Italian and Flemish pictures, part of which is intended for those apartments... It is to be hoped, when the palace is perfectly finished and furnished, that the King will order a catalogue and description of them, along with the plan and elevation of this magnificent fabrick, for the farther advancement of the polite arts and the satisfaction of those who love them ."

Joseph BARETTI: *Journey from London to Genoa, through England, Portugal, Spain and France* (in 1760). London, 1770.

Charles IV, like the console tables of carved and painted wood on which they stand.

Yellow Room

This room owes its name, and that of *Room of the Crowns* by which it was known in the 19th century, to the wall-hangings installed here on the instructions of Ferdinand VII; the walls are now covered by several panels of fabric woven at the Royal Factory from cartoons by José del Castillo under the direction of Francesco Sabatini, for the bedroom of Charles III. In addition to covering the walls, curtains for doors and balconies were also included, with coverings for the bed and bedspread, the chairs and other pieces of furniture, as well as for both sides of the fireplace screen, that here take the place of pelmets. The yellow silk framing the fabric panels was renewed in 1995.

Yellow Room. Secrétaire. Forestier and Thomire, c.1790.

Yellow Room. Fabric panel that once decorated the Bedroom of Charles III.

At the beginning of the reign of Charles III, this room was intended to be the Queen's Private Sitting Room, suggested by the topic of the fresco painted by Gian Domenico Tiepolo, *Juno in her Chariot*. From 1766 onwards, it was at the service of Charles III, who filled it with paintings by Teniers and Breughel, and excellent small portraits by Van Dyck and Velázquez. Remaining from that period is the socle of fine-wood marquetry made by German cabinetmakers from the workshop directed by Gasparini.

Ferdinand VII installed his bedroom here. He ordered Tiepolo's fresco to be erased, and Luis López to paint a new one, the theme of which is related to the new use of the room: Juno, on her golden chariot drawn by peacocks, and accompanied by Hymen, moves towards the place where Morpheus is sleeping.

The French furniture brought together here is the most outstanding of its type in the Palace. It was designed by Jean-Démosthène Dugourc,

Pedestal-table clock, after designs by J.D.Dugourc.

an important decorator who worked a great deal for Charles IV, first in France and later in Madrid, making items that mark the transition between the Louis XVI taste and the Empire style. Still within the former category are the chest-of-drawers and the secrétaire made around 1790 by Forestier and Thomire. The remaining pieces of furniture are characteristic of the "Etruscan style", in which Dugourc was a pioneer, a precursor of the Empire style. The sumptuous pedestal table, inspired by pieces of furniture found at Pompeii and Herculaneum, supports a horizontal clock made by Godon, with five circles indicating hours, months, calendar and weekly periods. The six chairs also follow archaeological models that are not in any way Spanish, despite the similarity of their back design to an ornamental hair-comb; they belong to a set made for the apartments of Queen María Luisa in the Palace of Aranjuez. Also dating to around 1800, but from Madrid, are the carpet from the Royal Factory, the two Buen Retiro vases, and the clock on the bureau, signed by Manuel Gutiérrez. The lamp is in the Ferdinand VII style (though it is not the one that was here at that time), as are the candelabra; the wall lamps date from the reign of Isabel II, when the King Consort, Francisco de Asís, had his dressing room here. From the time of Alfonso XII onwards, it has served as a sitting room and leads on to the Gala Dining Room.

THE QUEEN'S APARTMENTS: GALA DINING ROOM AND ADJACENT ROOMS

Gala Dining Room

The length of the great hall for balls and gala dinners is striking, since it is the result of joining together the three central rooms on the western façade. These rooms, and the three corresponding interior ones looking towards the main courtyard, during the reign of Charles III formed the Queen's apartments, intended for the Monarch's spouse who never occupied them since she died in 1760 before the Palace was in a habitable condition, but in fact used by the Queen Mother Isabella Farnese. The rooms facing onto the galleries served as antechambers. The last of these led to the room for luncheons and audiences, corresponding to the most distant section from the entrance door; the central area was the Chamber, and the closest one to the King's quarters was the bedroom, a logical arrangement allowing private passage between the apartments of the royal spouses.

Later occupied by the Infanta María Josefa and by the Princess of Asturias, this room was used again by the Queen during the reign of Ferdinand VII, who ordered important rehabilitation and redecoration work to be undertaken. Under Isabel II it was occupied by the King Consort Francisco de Asís, but when after the First Republic the Restoration returned the throne to the Bourbons, Alfonso XII wanted, instead of so many sets of apartments with large and medium-sized rooms and small studies, to have a large hall where gala banquets for more than one hundred people could be served. Therefore, in 1879 he commissioned his architect José Segundo de Lema to join these three rooms together, supporting the transversal walls on lowered arches, in

"The *Besamanos* is a terribly fussy and operose *función:* it is literally what it calls itself, and not only those who attend it, kiss hands, but every inmate of the palace, down to the porters and scullions…"
Mrs. William PITT BYRNE: *Things of Spain and the Spaniards as they are.* London, 1866.

Gala Dining Room.

such a way that both the structure and the decoration of the ceilings would remain intact. The work was not finished until 1885.

The architect succeeded in giving coherence to a space clearly sectioned into three parts and where the decoration of the ceilings is 18th-century, while on the walls the influence of the contemporary French neo-Baroque taste is evident in both the design, in which details of different origins (mainly Louis XVI) are brought together, and in the materials, since the columns are of Bagnères marble and most of the bronze work was executed in Paris, including the fifteen chandeliers and the ten wall lamps. Also from Paris are the chairs for a maximum number of one hundred and forty-four persons. The table has never been anything more than a frame without value as a piece of furniture, and it can be taken to pieces so that the room can also be used for balls.

For the decoration of the walls, the solution adopted was very much in line with the historicist taste of the epoch, the free spaces being covered with tapestries from the Royal Collection, forming part of the *Vertumnus and Pomona* series, woven at the end of the 16th century in Brussels by Pannemaker, from cartoons by Vermeyer. The

French fruit-bowl. 19th century. Glassware of Ferdinand VII.

Fresco on the central ceiling of the Gala Dining Room: Columbus offering the New World to Ferdinand and Isabel the Catholic. Antonio González Velázquez.

decoration of this room of King Alfonso XII is completed with twelve large 18th-century Chinese jars, and several large French 19th-century vases of gilded bronze and Sèvres porcelain, placed in the balcony recesses: six make up a series of historic scenes relating to the Kings of France and Spain, painted by Lachassagne and Renaud (1830), and the other two (beside the first and last balconies) have landscapes, from the middle of the century.

To conclude, it is worthwhile to examine the frescoes painted to decorate the Queen's apartments before the Dining Room was created. In the first section, where the bedroom used to be, the fresco is by Mengs, portraying *Aurora*. In 1880, the original stuccoes and other scenes by the same artist also on the ceiling were destroyed (they represented *The Four Moments of the Day* around the central scene), because for the sake of symmetry Sabatini's stucco decoration was copied, as it appears on the ceiling at the other end of the Dining Room. Another feature that disappeared was the frieze painted in the upper section of the walls by Langlois and Alejandro González Velázquez. Ferdinand VII had it decorated ostentatiously in the

"Turkish manner" as a "grand private sitting room of the Queen", with rich green damask draperies.

The fresco on the central vault corresponding to the Queen's Chamber, is by Antonio González Velázquez, and depicts Columbus offering the New World to the Catholic Monarchs, with four *chiaroscuro* medallions representing Mexico, Peru, Chile and the Philippine Islands. In 1818 Ferdinand VII decided on a great decorative scheme aimed at turning this room into the "Grand Boudoir" of the new Queen, his second wife María Isabel of Braganza: the fundamental pieces, besides the remarkable Empire-style furniture and the sumptuous orange silk drapery, were the six *chiaroscuro* paintings above the doorways, one of them by Goya, two by Vicente López and the other three by Zacarías G. Velázquez, Aparicio and Camarón. The presence of a work by Goya and the overall sense of unity gave this room an extraordinary importance.

The fresco on the last vault is by Francisco Bayeu; this was the "third antechamber" or "luncheon and royal audience room" of the Queen, and the fresco represents *Boabdil delivering the Keys of*

Fresco on the central ceiling of the Gala Dining Room: Boabdil delivering the keys of Granada to Ferdinand and Isabel the Catholic. Francisco Bayeu.

The ceremony of taking the cushion by the Lady Grandees of Spain was practically identical to that of covering Grandees, except for the symbol of their rank: to sit in front of the Queen, while all the other ladies remained standing.

"The Ladies take their places to the right (of the Queen) and have the cushion in front to sit on when the indication is given... Her Majesty says to the Ladies: *be seated*; to the Grandees: *be covered*... The Lady to take the cushion enters, with the sponsor to her right, leading her by the hand. Two steps from the entrance they make a curtsey to Her Majesty; half way across the room another, afterwards bowing to the Ladies and Grandees, who have risen from the cushion and removed their hats from the moment of the appearance at the door of those presenting themselves at the ceremony. Her Majesty says to the favoured Lady: *Be seated*... [after] a brief conversation the favoured Lady rises, kisses the Royal hand, and once again in the company of her sponsor, who returns to fetch her, bows to Her Majesty, and then to the other Ladies, and finally takes her seat on the first (cushion) of those that are unoccupied... At the end of the ceremony the Ladies stand up and Her Majesty walks around the circle...". Until well into the 18th century, women in Spain continued to sit on cushions on the floor, following the Moorish custom, which in the 19th century had passed out of use: "(Laughter sometimes bursts out), repressed on not a few occasions out of respect for Her Majesty, and caused by the difficulties experienced by some Ladies in sitting down and rising, which are contrary to the seriousness of the ceremony... making it necessary to have recourse to the mutual assistance which nowadays they give eachother...".
Guía Palaciana, Nº 12. Madrid, 1898.

Granada to the Catholic Monarchs. It is interesting that, in contrast to the mythological and allegorical themes dominating the other ceiling frescoes of the Palace, historical topics were chosen for the Queen's apartments, turning to the figure of Isabel the Catholic, in two of her most outstanding moments, as a reference point and inevitable model for any Spanish Sovereign. During the reign of Ferdinand VII this room was known as the Queen's Oratory, and under Isabel II, when it fulfilled the same role for the King Consort, the large circular couch which is now in the *Saleta* of Charles III was here.

Plateresque Room

Under Charles III this was the first of the Queen's antechambers. When the Gala Dining Room was created, Lema also modified the three rooms located between it and the main courtyard, in order to use them as relief, service and transit areas: he demolished all the partitions and ceilings that had divided it into smaller rooms during the reigns of Charles III and Charles IV, returning them to their original sizes, and he decorated the central one with pilasters and other architectural elements with motifs from the Spanish "plateresque" style, carved by Manuel Genné. Within the taste for using historical styles, this decoration is curious for such an early use of this national Renaissance repertoire rather than the Italian forms of the Quattrocento. The intention had been to gild the background of the carving to make it stand out more, but finally everything remained white, though beside a door a sample was left to show how the room would have looked with the use of varnish and gilding for the carving. This sudden interruption is explained by the death of Alfonso XII in 1885.

In the time of Alfonso XIII this room was used to project films for the Royal Family. At the present time an important Florentine table-centerpiece or *dessert* is displayed here; it is from the second half of the 18th century, but was enlarged in the Buen Retiro hard-stone workshops during the reign of Charles IV. Also in the room are six display cabinets containing some of the most important medals from the collection kept in the Royal Library, dating from the reign of Philip V to the present day.

Silverware Room

This was the second of the Queen's antechambers; as in the preceding and following ones, the alterations of Charles IV and Ferdinand VII led to the loss of the ceiling fresco, and in 1880 Lema also restored its original dimensions: it was he who installed here the elegant wood and marble socle. Currently, a selection of the domestic silverware used by the Royal Family is exhibited here. Joseph Bonaparte ordered all the older pieces to be melted down in order to support the cost of the war, and so the very rich eighteenth-century royal silverware was lost. Those items now on show are from the 19th century.

They include some made in the Martínez Silver Factory of Madrid, commissioned by Ferdinand VII for the Boudoir of Queen María Isabel of Braganza, in addition to many other pieces from the reigns of Isabel II and Alfonso XII and XIII. A detailed explanation is not given here

Reliquary of the Royal Chapel.

Preparatory sketch for one of the pilasters of the Plateresque Room. José Segundo de Lema. A.G.P.

because descriptions are provided in the show-cases. The religious silverware is in the Reliquary and in the adjacent strong-room of the Royal Chapel, and is not seen at the present time.

APARTMENTS OF THE INFANTE LUIS

The next three rooms visited were the first ones of the suite occupied from 1764 until his exile from the Court by the Infante Luis,

Fresco on the ceiling of the Stradivarius Room: Benignity accompanied by the Four Cardinal Virtues. Antonio González Velázquez.

brother of Charles III, and from 1785 onwards by the Infante Gabriel. In the reign of Isabel II they were assigned to the Duke and Duchess of Montpensier, and in the time of Alfonso XII and Alfonso XIII to the Infanta Isabel, known as "la Chata" (the snub-nosed).

In the first antechamber a selection of royal porcelain tableware is exhibited. Before the changes introduced by Ferdinand VII, this room had a ceiling fresco, *The Power of Spain in the Four Parts of the World*, ascribed by Fabre to Luis González Velázquez. During the reign of Alfonso XII it was the *Saleta* of the Infanta Isabel, from which time dates the present ceiling painting by the stage-set designers Busato and Bonardi.

Antechamber, or Stradivarius Room

Here are exhibited the quartet of instruments (viola, violoncello and two violins) made for the King of Spain by the celebrated Cremona luthier Antonio Stradivari, and purchased by Charles IV, and another violoncello by the same craftsman. In the centre of the room is a bronze model of the *Monument to Isabel the Catholic*, by Manuel Oms, inaugurated in Madrid's Paseo de la Castellana in 1883.

Quartet of viola, violoncello and two violins. Antonio Stradivari.

The ceiling retains the decoration of stucco and painting dating back to the reign of Charles III; the fresco portrays *Benignity accompanied by the Four Cardinal Virtues*, and it is the work of one of the González Velázquez brothers (Antonio according to Ponz and Ceán, or his brother Luis according to Fabre), Giaquinto's disciples. In those days this room was used for luncheons and audiences by the Infante Luis, and from 1785 onwards by the Infante Gabriel, who placed here the best pictures in his collection. Under Ferdinand VII it was the Queen's dining room, and later on the antechamber of Montpensier and the Infanta Isabel. The marble floor is from the time of Charles III, and it was moved from the adoining room when the Gala Dining Room was created in 1880, which was also the date of the wallpaper that has recently been rehung.

Chamber of the Infante Luis

The ceiling is admirably painted in fresco by Francisco Bayeu, who comes close to the quality of his master Mengs in this work, *Providence presiding over the Virtues and Faculties of Man*, the best of those that he undertook in the Palace. The wallpaper is new, but resembles a model from the reign of Ferdinand VII.

Several musical instruments from the 18th and 19th centuries are exhibited here, including the outstanding upright pianos shaped in imitation of bookshelves, built for Charles IV by Francisco Fernández (1805) and Francisco Flórez (1807); the one by Flórez is exquisitely decorated with bronzes, fine woods and painted crystal. Two pianos for children, one of them by Lesieur and the other by Rodrigo Ten (1918); some early nineteenth-century guitars; and two harps by Erard (1861). The Italian *stipo* follows the Florentine models typical of the 17th century, but it appears to be Milanese from the 19th century.

The people in the Palace.
Only on exceptional occasions did the people enter the royal apartments, as for example when the corpses of royal personages were lying in state: "After opening a path through the dense multitude surrounding the entrance [...] As foreigners we were allowed to pass without waiting in the queue with the multitude of *manolas* and *majos* [...] We were assigned a halberdier to accompany us, and at his presence a line was immediately formed, so that we could pass without difficulty up a great stone staircase and through a gallery where there was one of the most tightly-packed human agglomerations I have ever experienced. At last we reached a narrow door, where the press was even greater [...] Finally we reached the mortuory chamber. On a large four-poster bed lay the Prince of Asturias, embalmed and placed in a glass coffin. The Palace Guard was stationed around the walls, dressed in a handsome uniform somewhat similar to that of the *Garde Française*, blue with red trimmings [...] Magnificently robed priests were standing beside the royal corpse [...] but we did not have long to examine it all, as the Spaniards, pushing eachother, were passing by, and we were expected to do the same to leave room for the many persons desiring to see the corpse." H.Drummond WOLFF: *Madrilenia; or Pictures of Spanish Life*. London, 1851.

Detail of the ceiling fresco in the Chamber of the Infante Luis: Providence. Francisco Bayeu.

The remaining rooms of these apartments are small, and they are not visited. Their balconies overlook the Park and the gardens, and several of the ceilings have fresco paintings by González Velázquez, Maella, Bayeu and others, but outstanding among them is a charming one by Gian Domenico and Lorenzo Tiepolo, with many kinds of birds.

Chinaware Room

A selection from the most important services of tableware can be admired in this room: one belonging to Philip V, of *East India Company* porcelain; one of Charles III, commissioned from *Meissen* in 1738; and the one of the Prince and Princess of Asturias, Charles and María Luisa, made at *Sèvres* in 1776. Some consolation for the loss of so many of the eighteenth-century pieces is the abundance of those ordered from Paris by Ferdinand VII and Isabel II, especially the so-called landscape set from the Parisian manufacturers *Boin au Palais Royal*.

Plate with View of Burgos, from the landscape service. Boin.

MAIN GALLERY

The spacious corridor surrounding the courtyard at the level of the main floor allowed entry into the suites of each royal personage by way of their respective guard room or antechamber, thus being the main artery for the circulation of the courtiers. It was also accessible from the two general staircases communicating with the upper floors, known as the Cáceres and Ladies' Staircases, which are located in the northwest and northeast corners.

The architecture of the gallery is as it was conceived by Sacchetti, except that in his project the large windows would have been divided by stone jambs and lintels. Charles III ordered Sabatini to close them simply with large iron frames, as we see them now. He further gave instructions that the series of reliefs on political, military, scientific and religious subjects which Father Sarmiento had intended to place in panels above the windows, should not be installed; those that were made are now in the Prado Museum or the Academy of San Fernando.

Piece from the service of Philip V. East India Company.

Main Courtyard of the Palace.

Through any of the large windows one may contemplate the noble architecture of the courtyard, which is square, and slightly displaced to the North within the square shape of the Palace, since from the outset the architect had planned the southern range to be wider in order to accomodate the main staircase and the Chapel (which in the old Alcázar lay between the two courtyards of the King and the Queen). In order to emphasize the axis of the main entrance, Sacchetti made the central arches of the south and north sides wider, at the expense of narrowing the side arches, where are seen the four statues of Roman emperors that Charles III had removed from below the large balcony on the façade; Sabatini placed them here in 1791.

For great ceremonies the gallery was carpeted and the walls were covered with tapestries from the Royal Collection, so that the approach to the Chapel appeared more impressive.

Emperor Honorius. Giandomenico Olivieri.

Main Gallery.

"The gallery surrounding the courtyard, paved in marble, (is) always full of groups of guards and halberdiers on duty, and of people in Court dress who are to be presented to the Sovereign. This gallery gives access to the apartments of the different members of the Royal Family, the Chapel and the audience chamber."
Alexander Slidell MACKENZIE: *A year in Spain, by a young American.* London, 1831.

"The doors of a coved antechamber flew open, and after passing through an enfilade of saloons peopled with ladies-in-waiting and pages (some mere children), we entered a lofty chamber hung with white satin, formed into compartments by a rich embroidery of gold and coloured silks, and illuminated by a lustre of rock crystal".
William BECKFORD: *Italy; with sketches of Spain and Portugal...* (1787) London, 1834.

ROYAL CHAPEL

Sculptures of the Catholic Monarchs by José Vilches flank the doorway into the Royal Chapel. In 1742, due to criticism by Scotti, it was decided not to locate the Chapel as originally intended, where the Halberdiers' Room is now situated, but on its current site, by eliminating several of the rooms planned for the Infantes. After putting forward several options, always aimed at increasing the size of the Chapel, Sacchetti formulated his definitive plan in 1748, following which it was

Royal Chapel: The Coronation of the Virgin and other fresco paintings on sacred themes. Corrado Giaquinto.

"The Chapel-Royal is a gem of decoration, and rich in paintings and valuable marbles [...] the effect of the *tout ensemble* is gorgeous... Visitors are admitted by tickets to the high mass on Sundays [...] The appointed hour was twelve o'clock, and we were puntual to the time. We found the portion of the chapel reserved for strangers very crowded; but though there were many foreigners as usual, our party were the only representatives of our country. The grand staircase was thrown open, and the corridor, along which the royal family were to pass from the state chambers into the chapel, was carpeted [...] The sentinels walked up and down with the most solemn air, and two *Suisses,* or celadores, strutted about the entrance with most pavonic importance. The Chapel was carpeted, but in much more respectable style, and a really gorgeous daïs, and canopy, covered with cloth of gold, were prepared for the Queen and King Consort, with the royal arms embroidered in rich colours on the back; two thrones, with footstools and *prie-dieux* before them stood on the daïs".
Mrs. William PITT BYRNE: *Things of Spain. Illustrative of Spain and the Spaniards as they are.* London, 1866.

"As the King was staying at the palace [...] we could not see the rooms; but had to content ourselves with looking at His Majesty's private chapel, where a service was going on. The organ is very superior to the generality of Spanish instruments, and occasionally delivered itself of very striking sounds".
Zouch Horace TURTON: *To the desert and back; or, Travels in Spain, the Barbary States, Italy, etcetera, in 1875-1876.* London, 1876.

built exactly as it is today. Nevertheless, the decoration was never completed according to the ideas of the architect, who had planned for the floors and all the walls to be of marble, and for the capitals and bases of the columns and pilasters to be of bronze. Moreover, neither the altarpieces, nor the form of the screen (enclosing the glazed gallery at the west end of the Chapel, destined for use by the Monarchs) and the choir, follow Sacchetti's final proposal. Charles III ordered the Chapel to be completed "provisionally" in stucco, as it appears nowadays, since he planned to extend it by adding a projection towards the north, for which Sabatini prepared two projects that were never put into effect.

The decoration proposed by Sacchetti, with the collaboration of Ventura Rodríguez and Corrado Giaquinto, if it ever had been completed, would have achieved a magnificence difficult to equal. Of this scheme, what was carried out is the whole decoration of the ceilings, and the ten large columns made from single pieces of black marble from Mañaria (Basque Country).

From the cornice upwards, everything is by Giaquinto: his are the designs of the stuccoes, painted by Andreoli, and again his are the grandiose frescoes representing *St.James at Clavijo* above the entrance doorway, *Glory, with the Holy Trinity Crowning the Virgin* in the dome, and in the pendentives Saints *Isidoro, Hermenegildo, Isidro Labrador and María de la Cabeza; The Holy Trinity* in the gallery behind the altar, which was to have been placed further back, and in the choir *Allegory of Religion*. The angels are by Felipe de Castro, except for those flanking the eucharistic symbol, which are by Olivieri.

Royal Chapel. Throne canopy.

Royal Chapel. Altarpiece of The
Annunciation. Anton Raphael Mengs.

In comparison to the sumptuous effect of the vaults, the picture
over the high altar is very modest: *St.Michael* by Ramón Bayeu after an
original by Giordano and a drawing by his master Mengs. Precisely
Mengs was responsible for the *Annunciation*, his last work, left
unfinished at his death in Rome in 1779. The architecture of both
altarpieces is by Sabatini, except for the table of the Annunciation, by
Isidro Velázquez, containing the relics of the Roman martyr St.Felix.
The sculptures of the Sacred Hearts are by Juan Samsó, and those of
the Four Evangelists in the Ante-Chapel by José Ginés.

"Everything about the Madrid Alcazar is grand, if not strictly beautiful [...] a stately entrance to the somewhat too gorgeous suite of state apartments; everything on a large scale, and befitting a grand imperial residence." Antonio C. N. GALLENGA *Iberian reminiscences. Fifteen years' travelling impressions of Spain and Portugal.* London, 1883.

Terrace overlooking Main Courtyard.

In addition to the daily worship conducted by a numerous body of Chaplains, at whose head was the Cardinal Patriarch of the Indies, His Majesty's Almoner and Principal Chaplain, the solemn ceremonies were undertaken with great pomp. Usually, the King and other members of the Royal Family would follow the service from the screen or glazed gallery at the west end of the Chapel reached from the interior of the royal apartments, but on solemn feast days the Sovereign would come out in procession by way of the gallery around the courtyard decked out with tapestries. On reaching the Chapel he would bow before the altar, and then again before the Queen who was standing at the screen, then occupying his seat of honour beneath the canopy. Every member of the Court had a place assigned: directly beside the King were the Chamberlain of the Palace and the Captain of the Royal Guard, then the Grandees facing the door, and so on. The public was only allowed to occupy the entrance section, or Ante-Chapel.

Ferdinand VI wished for a sumptuous though not particularly large Chapel, and so he aimed at splendour in all the details, including the numerous liturgical vestments (particularly the cope bearing his name), the choir books and the organ, since music was of great importance to this Monarch, as it had been to his father, and the Royal Chapel had a numerous yet select group of instrumentalists and singers. The organ, with a case designed by Ventura Rodríguez, was begun by Leonardo Fernández Dávila and finished by Jorge Bosch, from Mallorca. It is unique in Spain due not only to its intrinsic quality, but also because it escaped any modification in the nineteenth century. It has recently been scrupulously restored.

GUARD ROOM AND BACK ROOMS OF QUEEN MARÍA LUISA

Guard Room of Queen María Luisa

This room provided access to the apartments occupied by María Luisa of Parma from 1765 until 1808, first as Princess of Asturias, and then from 1788 onwards as Queenn (see page 69). Now it contains pieces from the reign of Ferdinand VII, including the outstanding neoclassical *dessert* or table-centre in marble and bronze, and the round table with a small temple, a French work in gilded and blued bronze, malachite and granite, with sculptures of *Apollo and the Nine Muses*. The portraits of *Louis Philippe of Orleans, King of France*, and his wife *María Amalia of the Two Sicilies*, gifts to Isabel II, are by F. X. Winterhalter, and that of Francis I of the Two Sicilies by Vicente López.

The three remaining paintings are from other periods. Earlier in time, dated in 1693, are the pair of *Miracles of San Eloy* by the Madrid artist Isidoro Arredondo (they once formed part of the collection of the Marqués de Salamanca, and came frome the old Parish Church of San Salvador, in the Plaza de la Villa of Madrid). Later, dated 1886, is the *Alfonso XII* by Federico de Madrazo: like the one painted slightly earlier by Casado del Alisal, this was an official posthumous portrait, which in part explains the Bourbon blue colour of the eyes.

*Royal Chapel. High Altar and
Throne Dais.*

*Design for the Billiard Room. José
Segundo de Lema. A.G.P.*

Billiard Room of Alfonso XII

We return to the main gallery and from there enter the first of this suite of María Luisa of Parma's "back-rooms", the name given in the Palace to those rooms in the royal quarters that did not look towards the façades but were interior or received light from the courtyard; they were kept for relaxation and private moments aside from the routine of Court life. The ceiling of this room has a fresco painting by Mariano Salvador Maella (1769), with a mythological scene, *Juno ordering Aeolus to unleash the Winds against Aeneas*. It is undoubtedly the best work in this genre done

Billiard Room.

Magnificence.
"The first view of the exterior conveys an idea of magnificence ... The interior of the building compensates for the external faults, being excelled by no palace in Europe in splendour and elegance... Those [the apartments] of the Queen, which we next entered, are on a much grander scale, extending the whole length of the palace, and communicating with each other, so that when the folding doors are thrown open, the eye is almost dazzled by the splendid elegance of a long suite of magnificent saloons [...] In short, every thing is so magnificent, as to shut out all idea of comfort: the eye is dazzled, the mind struck with admiration, but neither is pleased. For my own part, the reflection I made was, how miserable I should be if forced to inhabit these superb apartments! For I am so unambitious as to prefer a well polished snug mahogany table, a good fire, and the society of a few friends, to grandeur accompanied by ceremony and formality, which must have been always the case here, as none ever entered these apartments but in full dress, and with a feeling of their own inferiority" .
Andrew Thomas, Lord BLAYNEY: *Narrative of a forced journey through Spain and France as a prisoner of war in the years 1810 to 1814.*

by this artist, who was still young at the time and who later was perhaps over-prolific, but it is hidden by the wooden coffered ceiling designed by J.S. de Lema when in 1879 Alfonso XII had him build a Billiard Room here: following English Victorian examples and the rationalist derivation of Gothic motifs produced by Viollet-le-Duc, Lema worked here in a manner characteristic of his style and of the taste prevailing in those years; it is perfectly coherent and not without charm, being completed in 1881 and restored in 1993. The joinery and carving of the walnut panelling is by Antonio Girón, as are the other furnishings except for the table, which is from Paris. The doorway through which this room is entered dates from the above changes; until then its place was occupied by a window.

Smoking Room of Alfonso XII
Near the Billiard Room the King wished for a Smoking Room decorated in the "Chinese" manner. Lema covered the walls

with porcelain plaques ordered from the Boulanger Factory, at Choisy-le-Roi (Paris), and with embroidered silk fabrics, as seen nowadays following the restoration of 1993; the ensemble had been removed after 1939 due to damage from bombardments during the Civil War. However, it was decided not to replace the ceiling, which was decorated in a similar manner, so as to reveal the eighteenth-century stucco-work and the tempera painting by Joaquín Espalter, dating from 1857.

Smoking or Japanese Room. Detail.

Queen María Luisa's Plasterwork Room

Despite its small dimensions, this neoclassical private sitting-room is one of the most fascinating rooms in the Palace. It was designed by Francesco Sabatini and the stucco work is by the Brilli brothers, who found inspiration in the archaeological repertoire of Pompeii then in vogue.

Design for Billiard Room. José Segundo de Lema. A.G.P.

Queen María Luisa's Fine-Woods Room

In evident contrast to the previous room, this private study in the Rococo taste and its furniture (a bureau, two chests-of-drawers, an armchair and two seats) were made by Gasparini's team of

Detail of the Plasterwork Room.

Plasterwork Room.

cabinetmakers and bronzesmiths. It seems to have been one of the private rooms of Charles III, which was dismantled and removed from its original place and adapted to this space in the time of Charles IV. Although the style was already very old-fashioned, the sumptuousness of the work was worthy of the Queen; the design of the flooring and the ceiling stuccoes is by G.B. Ferroni.

Rooms which are not visited. The Royal Library

Queen María Luisa's Fine-Woods Room.

Rooms of Queen María Luisa and Charles IV

These back rooms formed part of the Queen's apartments, the front balconies of which overlook the Plaza de Oriente. Beyond them, the rooms of Charles IV also give onto this square and to the Parade Ground. Of all these rooms that are not open to the public, due to the frequent use made of them by His Majesty the King for his military and civil audiences and other official functions, those particularly worthy of mention are: Queen María Cristina's *Saleta*, with furniture from the time of Charles IV; the *Daily Dining Room*, with architectural decoration by Sabatini; *Queen María Luisa's Boudoir*, also known as the Hall of Mirrors, an exquisite piece of work by the same architect and the same stucco plasterers as the little Plasterwork Room; the *Tapestry Room*, which takes its name from the tapestries on the *History of Joseph, David and Solomon* that decorate it; the *Weapons Room*, with 16th century tapestries; and the *Chamber*, with large console tables from the reign of Charles III. The ceilings of all these rooms have fresco paintings by F. Bayeu and M. S. Maella, that of the Antechamber by Gian Domenico Tiepolo, and that of the *Saleta* by Gian Battista Tiepolo.

Tabletop of Florentine mosaic in the rooms once belonging to Queen María Luisa.

Frieze of Queen María Luisa's Fine-Woods Room. Detail.

"This palace, whether it be viewed with reference to its architecture or decoration, is, indeed, a noble one. I have heard it said, by those who had visited the chief capitals of Europe, that they had seen none superior to it, and, though Versailles may excel in detail, as a perfect whole the palace of Madrid may even claim preeminence".
Alexander Slidell MACKENZIE: *A year in Spain, by a young American.* London 1831.

Former Library of Charles IV, subsequently private rooms of the Monarchs in the 19th and 20th centuries.

For the same reasons, there are also no visits to the rooms housed in the St.Giles Wing (between the Parade Ground and Calle Bailén) entered from the Chamber of Charles IV, where this King had his Library, and Isabel II and her successors had their private rooms. The ceilings make up a unitary group of stuccoes and paintings executed between 1784 and 1787, the stuccoes according to Sabatini's designs and the fresco paintings by Bayeu and Maella. The decoration and the furniture correspond to the last period when these rooms were inhabited, during the reign of Alfonso XIII, but include some pieces of great interest from earlier times. There are some remarkable items of 18th-century French and Spanish furniture, a fine-wood cabinet by Gasparini and chandeliers from the period of Ferdinand VII.

Mirror with effigy of Charles III, made at the Royal Crystal Factory of San Ildefonso c.1775, from a portrait by Anton Raphael Mengs. Royal Library.

Of how the Palace, without growing, becomes large.
"When the Bourbons were reigning the entire Palace was occupied: the King lived in the part on the left, towards the Plaza de Oriente; Queen Isabel II in the part facing the Plaza de Oriente on one side and the Plaza de la Armería on the other; Montpensier in the part opposite that of the Queen; each of the Princes had a room facing the gardens of the Campo del Moro. *[It was the opposite: the King Consort in the rooms of Charles III and in those of the western façade, where the Gala Dining Room is now situated; and the Infantas in the rooms on the east. The wing with the private rooms of Isabel II was the one also occupied later by Alfonso XIII].*
During the time that King Amadeus was there, a large part of the building remained empty. He had only three small rooms: one little study, a bedroom and a dressing room. The bedroom gave onto a long passage leading to the rooms of the Princes, beside which were the quarters of the Queen, who never wanted to be separated from her children. There was also a room used for receptions. All this part which served for the entire Royal Family had previously been occupied by Queen Isabel alone. When she heard that King Amadeus and Queen Victoria had satisfied themselves with such a small space, she is said to have exclaimed in astonishment: Poor young things, they won't be able to move!".
Edmondo de AMICIS: *España. Viaje durante el reinado de D.Amadeo I.* Florence, 1872.

The Royal Library

The Private Royal Library or His Majesty's Chamber Library, as it was called in the 18th century, is not included in the tour. It is located on the lower floor since María Cristina de Borbón had it moved from the main floor to occupy its space with private quarters; its rooms, with bookshelves from the period of Isabel II and Alfonso XII, have a great deal of character, and the collections of manuscripts and of old printed texts are very important, in addition to the wealth of illuminated manuscripts and bindings held there. In the mornings it offers an excellent place for research to be undertaken.

Hall of Mirrors, formerly the Boudoir of Queen Maria Luisa of Parma. Decorative stuccoes. Giuseppe and Domenico Brilli, under the direction of Francesco Sabatini.

Main Vestibule, with the statue of
Charles III opposite the Staircase.
Pierre Michel.

Main Vestibule. Detail.

THE LOWER FLOOR

From the Main Vestibule, where the gift-shop is located, one goes out to the Small Vestibule of Charles III: the large doorway opposite leads to the suite known since 1924 as the Genoa Rooms. During the *Ancien Régime* the Ministry of State occupied this area; beyond were the War and Navy Ministries, following the gallery around the main courtyard, at the rear of which was the Ministry of Grace and Justice (where the Library is now situated). Then came the Ministry for the Indies, at the end of the far gallery which continues to the small vestibule of the Chamberlain's Office, opposite the main entrance. Finally, access to the Finance Ministry was by the current entrance to the offices of Patrimonio Nacional beside the Parade Ground. Thus, the essential administrative activity of the vast Spanish Monarchy at the moment of its maximum territorial extension was housed on this floor of the Palace.

Roundel of The Medusa. Royal Armoury.

"The distant hills beyond the river have a wild, uncultivated, but rather grand appearance; and in the distance, the fine range of the Guadarrama, covered with snow, is such a view as is certainly not enjoyed from a royal palace in any other metropolis; and fortunately it is not spoilt by any straggling, ugly suburbs. "
G.A. HOSKINS: *Spain, as it is.* London, 1851.

Equestrian armour of Charles V. Royal Armoury.

To reach the Royal Armoury, one goes out to the Parade Ground and follows the gallery of arches on the right, passing the doorway of the *General Palace Archive* (the most important one in Madrid after the National Historic Archive), with a chance to look out over the landscape extending away as far as the Guadarrama Mountains.

ROYAL ARMOURY

This is the most important armoury in Europe together with the Imperial Armoury in Vienna, due both to the quality of its pieces and the history that confers meaning on such a Collection of Arms, basically intended for gala displays. Philip II ordered it to be moved here and installed in a building that bore this same name and used to stand where the railing enclosing the Parade Ground is now situated.

The present building, containing a large hall, was designed by the architects J.S. de Lema and E. Repullés, and was inaugurated in 1897. The Collection has been open to the public for over four centuries. The existence of a specific guide-book to the Arms Collection makes it unnecessary to provide any further information here.

Main façade of the Palace. Axis with one of the doorways leading to the small vestibules.

"It appeared to me a much handsomer building than the Tuilleries. One always looks upon it with renewed pleasure; for it leaves upon the mind that impression of gracefulness combined with strength, which are the essential attributes of beauty. "
Michael Joseph QUINN: *A visit to Spain... in the latter part of 1822 and the first months of 1823.*

Royal Pharmacy. Baroque herbarium.

ROYAL PHARMACY

The range of buildings on the opposite side of the Parade Ground houses the Royal Pharmacy, which used to supply medicines to the Royal Family and all the employees and staff of the Royal Household.

The Palace from the Plaza de Oriente. Equestrian statue of Philip IV. Pietro Tacca.

The Palace as a labyrinth.
"It is composed of three stories underground, and five above-ground. The rooms (or cellars) of the lower story under ground ... [are] to serve as a repository of the eatables. The kitchens will take up the story over it; and over the kitchens all the people employed in them will be lodged. Those three stories are so well contrived, that even the lowermost is not totally deprived of light ... If the underground apartments are grand, you may easily think that those above-ground cannot be mean. Those on the ground-floor are already inhabited by some of the great officers at court. The King's apartments are over those of the great officers... and the fourth and fifth occupied by their attendants."
Joseph BARETTI: *Journey from London to Genoa, through England, Portugal Spain and France* (in 1760). London, 1770.

Royal Pharmacy. One of set of jars.

In the entrance and corridor there are several large 18th-century Talavera-ware jars. In the first room on the right are displayed sets of pots and shelving from the pharmacy of the former General Hospital of Madrid, also going back to the end of the 18th century. Then, in the second room, are sets of 18th-century jars from the Royal Pharmacy itself. The third room contains a set of 19th-century porcelain jars, and in the fourth room are 19th-century jars of La Granja crystal. In the last room is a reconstruction of an ancient pharmaceutical "office".

SURROUNDINGS OF THE PALACE

The Palace from Calle de Bailén, with the Sabatini Gardens.

The exterior of the Palace. Plaza de Oriente. Sabatini Gardens. the Park Gardens or "Campo del Moro"

The *Plaza de la Armería*, inserted between the railings and the new Cathedral, is narrow and therefore does not offer a perspective of the Royal Palace as distant and impressive as it would have been if it were not for the triumph, under Alfonso XII, of the idea of using this site (intended since the time of Sacchetti to become a Parade Forecourt) to build the Cathedral of La Almudena, which was finally completed in 1992.

Therefore, in order to enjoy the admirable prospect offered by the Palace from a distance, it is necessary to go to the *Plaza de Oriente*, an

open space created under Joseph Bonaparte by demolishing several buildings of the Royal Household. The site was definitively laid out and landscaped under Isabel II, when the monument with the magnificent *Equestrian Statue of Philip IV* (by the Florentine sculptor Pietro Tacca) was placed in the centre, opposite the Prince's Gate into the Palace.

From Calle de Bailén, a flight of steps descends to the *Gardens of Sabatini*, created during the Second Republic on the site of the Royal Stables built by Sabatini on the instructions of Charles III. The northern façade of the Palace displays here the full height of its various storeys and the Royal Chapel dome.

From these gardens, a ramp goes down to the *Paseo de San Vicente*, and following the wrought-iron railings as far as the *Paseo de la Virgen del Puerto*, one reaches the entrance to the Palace Park, popularly known as the *Campo del Moro* (the Moor's Field). The creation of this historic garden was due to Philip II, and it is agreeable though what now exists is less interesting than what was never built. This is because in the 18th century several projects were drawn up, amongst which those of Sacchetti and Ventura Rodríguez, and one commissioned in 1747 from Esteban Boutelou (head gardener at Aranjuez) and Garnier de l'Isle (the Superintendant of Versailles), are specially noteworthy. None of them was ever executed, nor was one by Sabatini (1767), but instead it was necessary to wait until the reign of Isabel II, when the project of Narciso Pascual y Colomer (1844) was begun; the design of its main rectilinear avenues still survives, as do the two fountains alined on the central axis, the *Fountain of the Shells* (by Felipe de Castro and Manuel Alvarez, 1775) brought from the palace of the Infante Luis at Boadilla del Monte, and that of the *Tritons*, an Italian work of the 16th century, brought here from the Islet Garden at Aranjuez and situated in front of the "large grotto" or hothouse. Finally, during the regency of María Cristina of Habsburg, the park was totally reformed according to a pseudo-landscape design by Ramón Oliva (1890).

The splendid view of Sacchetti's building from the central avenue of the Garden invites us to seek its most spectacular aspect from a more distant point, on the ancient royal property of the *Casa de Campo* or from the *Montaña del Príncipe Pío*. Indeed, it is from this perspective that one comes to understand this Royal Palace.

The Palace from the Park or Campo del Moro, with the Fountain of the Shells.

The Palace in the Madrid landscape.

"Seen from the old Castile highway, from the banks of the Manzanares, from the Estación del Norte or from the Montaña del Príncipe Pío, this Palace has an imposing appearance, elevated on great retaining walls and buttresses, the terraces and sloping gardens forming a magnificent pedestal, and with its white mass cut out against this beautiful sky in the most picturesque manner..."
A.GERMOND DE LAVIGNE: *Itinéraire descriptif, historique et littéraire de Madrid...* Paris, 1859.

"The Royal Palace, with architecture at once rich and severe, points two of its four faces towards the countryside, so that it is necessary to go down with little convenience to the depths of a species of abyss in order to be able to contemplate the most notable of its façades, if you wish to appreciate its position; the main façade faces onto a large square into which no important street runs; the fourth and last of its sides is the only one that can be seen from the Plaza de Oriente, and even there the perspective is no longer enjoyed as soon as you plunge into one of the neighbouring streets."
Marie Studolmine RATAZZI: *L'Espagne moderne*. Paris, 1879.

"The Palace of Madrid is a splendid building [...]The east front is very handsome and imposing, and the west side is also magnificent; a noble and very extensive inclined drive, reminding me in form of the approach to the Monte Pincio, in Rome, leads up to a noble terrace before the Palace".
HOSKINS, G.A. *Spain, as it is*. London, 1851.

BIBLIOGRAPHY

Alcázar of Madrid

ORSO, Steven N.: *In the presence of the Planet King: Philip IV and the decoration of the Alcázar of Madrid.* Princeton University Press 1986 (revision of doctoral thesis, 1978).

GERARD, Véronique: *De castillo a Palacio. El Alcázar de Madrid en el siglo XVI.* Madrid, Xarait, 1984 (contains the earlier bibliography).

BARBEITO, José: *El Alcázar de Madrid.* Doctoral thesis defended in the Architecture School, Universidad Politécnica de Madrid, 1988. Published by C.O.A.M., Madrid 1992.

Various Authors: *El Real Alcázar de Madrid.* Exhibition Catalogue, by Fernando Checa Cremades. Comunidad de Madrid, 1994.

Guide-Book

NIÑO MAS, Felipe, and JUNQUERA DE VEGA, Paulina: *Guía ilustrada del Palacio Real de Madrid*, Patrimonio Nacional. Madrid, 1956, 3rd ed. This Guide is available in corrected and expanded editions of 1966, by M. López Serrano, and 1985, by F. Fernández Miranda y Lozana.

General

AGUEDA VILLAR, Mercedes: *Antonio Rafael Mengs 1728-1799.* Exhibition Catalogue, Museo del Prado, Madrid, 1980.

ANDRADA, Ramón: "Las estatuas del Palacio de Oriente vuelven a su sitio", *R.S.*, 1972, 9, N° 31, pp. 49-56.

ANDRADA, Ramón: "Obras de reconstrucción en el Palacio de Oriente", *R.S.*, 1965, 2, N° 3, pp. 70-75.

Apollo, LXXXVI, N° 75, London, May 1968: Special Number on the Royal Palace of Madrid.

BARRENO SEVILLANO, Mª Luisa: "Pontifical bordado. Capilla del Palacio Real de Madrid", *R.S.*, 1978, 15, N° 56, pp. 17-28.

BARRENO SEVILLANO, Mª Luisa: "Salón de Gasparini o pieza de la parada", *R.S.*, 1975, 12, N°43, pp.61-72.

BENITO GARCIA, Pilar: "Los textiles y el mobiliario del Palacio Real de Madrid", *R.S.*, 1991, 28, N° 109, pp. 45-60.

BOTTINEAU, Yves: *L'Art de Cour dans l'Espagne de Philippe V*, Bordeaux 1962. Spanish ed., *El arte cortesano en la España de Felipe V (1700-1746)*, Madrid, F.U.E., 1986. New French edition, corrected and expanded, Société des amis du Musée de Sceaux, Paris 1992.

BOTTINEAU, Yves: *L'Art de Cour dans l'Espagne des Lumières*, Paris, De Boccard, 1986.

CABEZA GIL-CASARES, Carmen: "Bordados del salón de Gasparini", *R.S.*, 1992, 29, N° 114, pp.12-28.

CABEZA GIL-CASARES, Carmen, and SANCHO, José Luis: "La restauración de las salas de billar y de fumar en el P.R.M., la recuperación de un conjunto alfonsino", in *R.S.*, N° 118 (1993).

CHECA CREMADES, Fernando: "Los frescos del Palacio Real Nuevo de Madrid y el fin del lenguaje alegórico", *Archivo Español de Arte*, LXV, 258 (1992), pp.157-178, with complete up-dated bibliography.

COLON DE CARVAJAL, José Ramón: *Catálogo de Relojes del Patrimonio Nacional.* P.N., Madrid 1987.

CUMBERLAND, R., *An accurate and descriptive Catalogue of the several paintings in the King of Spain's Palace at Madrid*, London, 1787.

DURAN SALGADO, Miguel: *Exposición de proyectos no realizados relativos al Palacio de Oriente y sus jardines*. Madrid, 1935.

ECHALECU, J. Mª, "Los talleres reales de ebanistería, bronces y bordados", *Archivo Español de Arte*. 1955, Vol. XXVIII, pp. 237-259.

ESPOZ Y MINA, Condesa de (Juana Vega de Mina): *Apuntes para la historia del tiempo en que ocupó los destinos de aya de S.M. y A. y camarera mayor de Palacio su autora -*. Madrid 1910.

FABRE, Francisco José: *Descripción de las Alegorías pintadas en las bóvedas del Real Palacio de Madrid, hecha de orden de S.M. por ...*, Madrid, Aguado, 1829.

FEDUCHI, Luis M: *Colecciones reales de España: el mueble*. Patrimonio Nacional, Madrid 1965.

FEDUCHI, Luis M.: *El mueble en España. Volúmenes I y II: El Palacio Nacional*. Madrid, Afrodisio Aguado, 1949.

GARCIA MERCADAL, J., *Viajes de extranjeros por España y Portugal*. Recopilación, traducción, prólogo y notas por -. Aguilar, Madrid, 1962.

GOMEZ MOLINERO, Encarnación, and SANCHEZ HERNANDEZ, Leticia: "El botamen de cristal de la Real Farmacia. Nuevos datos para su estudio", *R.S.*, 1987, 24, Nº93, pp. 33-36.

GOMEZ DE LAS HERAS, *El Palacio Real de Madrid*, Madrid 1935.

GRITELLA, Gianfranco: *Juvarra. L'Architettura*. Modena, 1992, Vol. II, ficha 124.

IGLESIAS, Helena (dir.): *El Palacio Real de Madrid: un recorrido a través de su arquitectura*. Dibujos de los alumnos de la II Cátedra de Análisis de Formas Arquitectónicas de la ETSAM. Patrimonio Nacional, 1990.

JUNQUERA, Juan José: *La decoración y el mobiliario en los palacios de Carlos IV*. Madrid, 1979.

JUNQUERA, Paulina: "Los libros de coro de la Real Capilla", *R.S.*, 1965, 2, Nº6, pp. 12-27.

JUNQUERA, Paulina: "Muebles franceses con porcelanas en el Palacio de Oriente", *R.S.*, 1966, 3, Nº8, pp. 28-37.

JUNQUERA DE VEGA, Paulina, and HERRERO CARRETERO, Concha: *Catálogo de tapices del Patrimonio Nacional*. Vol. 1: siglo XVI. P.N., Madrid 1986.

JUNQUERA DE VEGA, Paulina, y DIAZ GALLEGOS, Carmen: *Catálogo de tapices del Patrimonio Nacional*. Vol. II: siglo XVII. P.N., Madrid 1986.

LOPEZ SERRANO, Matilde (ed.): *El palacio Real de Madrid*, Patrimonio Nacional, Madrid, 1975.

MARTIN, Fernando A.: *Catálogo de la plata del Patrimonio Nacional*. P.N., Madrid 1987.

MORALES Y MARIN, José Luis: *Mariano Salvador Maella*, Madrid 1992.

MORALES Y MARIN, José Luis: *Vicente López (1772-1850)*, Exhibition Catalogue. Madrid, 1990.

MORALES Y MARIN José Luis: *Los Bayeu*, Zaragoza, 1979.

MORAN TURINA, Juan Miguel: *La imagen del Rey. Felipe V y el arte*, Madrid, 1990.

PEREZ VILLAAMIL, M., *Artes e industrias del Buen Retiro*. Madrid, 1904.

PEREZ GALDOS, Benito: *La de Bringas*. Madrid, 1884. Ed. Hernando, Madrid.

PLAZA SANTIAGO, Francisco Javier de la: *Investigaciones sobre el Palacio Real Nuevo de Madrid*, Valladolid 1975. For now this is the fundamental study. It includes all the earlier bibliography.

PONZ, Antonio: *Viaje de España*, XVIII volumes, Madrid, 1769-1793. Vol.6. 3rd printing, Madrid, Ibarra 1793.

REYERO, Carlos: "Isabel II y la pintura de historia", *R.S.*, 1991, 28, Nº 107, pp. 28-36.

RUIZ ALCON, Mª Teresa: "Habitaciones y objetos personales del rey don Alfonso XIII en el museo del Palacio Real de Madrid", *R.S.*, 1980, 17, Nº 63, pp. 17-28.

SANCHEZ HERNANDEZ, Leticia: "La vajilla de paisajes del Patrimonio Nacional conservada en el Palacio Real de Madrid", *R.S.*, 1985, 22, Nº 83, pp. 37-52.

SANCHEZ HERNANDEZ, Mª Leticia: *Catálogo de porcelana y cerámica española del Patrimonio Nacional en los Palacios Reales*. P.N., Madrid 1989.

SANCHO, José Luis: "Sacchetti y los salones del Palacio Real de Madrid", *R.S.*, 1988, 25, Nº 96, pp. 37-44.

SANCHO, José Luis: "Proyectos del siglo XVIII para los jardines del Palacio de Madrid: Esteban Boutelou y Garnier de l'Isle", *Anales del Instituto de Estudios Madrileños*, Vol.XXV (1988), pp. 403-433.

SANCHO, José Luis: "El Palacio Real de Madrid. Alternativas y críticas a un proyecto". *Reales Sitios*, Special Number (1989), pp. 167-180.

SANCHO, José Luis: "El piso principal del Palacio Real", *Reales Sitios*, Nº 109 (1991).

SANCHO, José Luis: "Fernando Fuga, Nicola Salvi y Luigi Vanvitelli; el Palacio Real de Madrid y sus escaleras principales", in *Storia dell'Arte*, Roma, Nº 72 (1991), pp. 199-252.

SANCHO, José Luis: "Las críticas en España y desde Italia al Palacio Real de Madrid", *Archivo Español del Arte*, Nº 254 (1991), pp. 201-254.

SANCHO, José Luis: "Espacios para la Majestad en el siglo XVIII: la distribución de las habitaciones reales en el Palacio Nuevo de Madrid". *Anales del Instituto de Estudios Madrileños*, Vol.XXXI, Madrid 1992, pp. 19-40.

SANCHO, José Luis: "Francisco Sabatini, **primer arquitecto**, director de la decoración interior de los palacios reales", article on pp. 143-166; and notes on interior decoration pp. 227-236, pp. 236-240, pp. 241-244; all in Var.Auth.: *Francisco Sabatini, la arquitectura como metáfora del poder*, Exhibition Catalogue, Madrid 1993.

SANCHO, José Luis: *La arquitectura de los Sitios Reales. Catálogo histórico de los Palacios, jardines y Patronatos Reales del Patrimonio Nacional*. Patrimonio Nacional-Fundación Tabacalera, Madrid 1995. With complete bibliography and plans.

TARRAGA BALDO, Mª Luisa: *G.D.Olivieri y el taller de escultura del Palacio Real*. Patrimonio Nacional, C.S.I.C. and Istituto Italiano di Cultura, Madrid, 1992.

TORMO 1927: TORMO, Elías: *Las iglesias del antiguo Madrid*. Madrid,1927. Republished by Instituto de España. Madrid 1972.

TURMO, Isabel: *Museo de carruajes*. Patrimonio Nacional, 1969.

R.S.: *Reales Sitios*, magazine of Patrimonio Nacional.

THIS BOOK WAS PRINTED ON THE 18TH DAY OF APRIL 1998, FESTIVITY OF SAN PERFECTO, CO-EDITED BY PATRIMONIO NACIONAL AND ALDEASA AND PRINTED AT ESTUDIOS GRAFICOS EUROPEOS, MADRID